TECHNIQUES FOR COMMUNICATORS

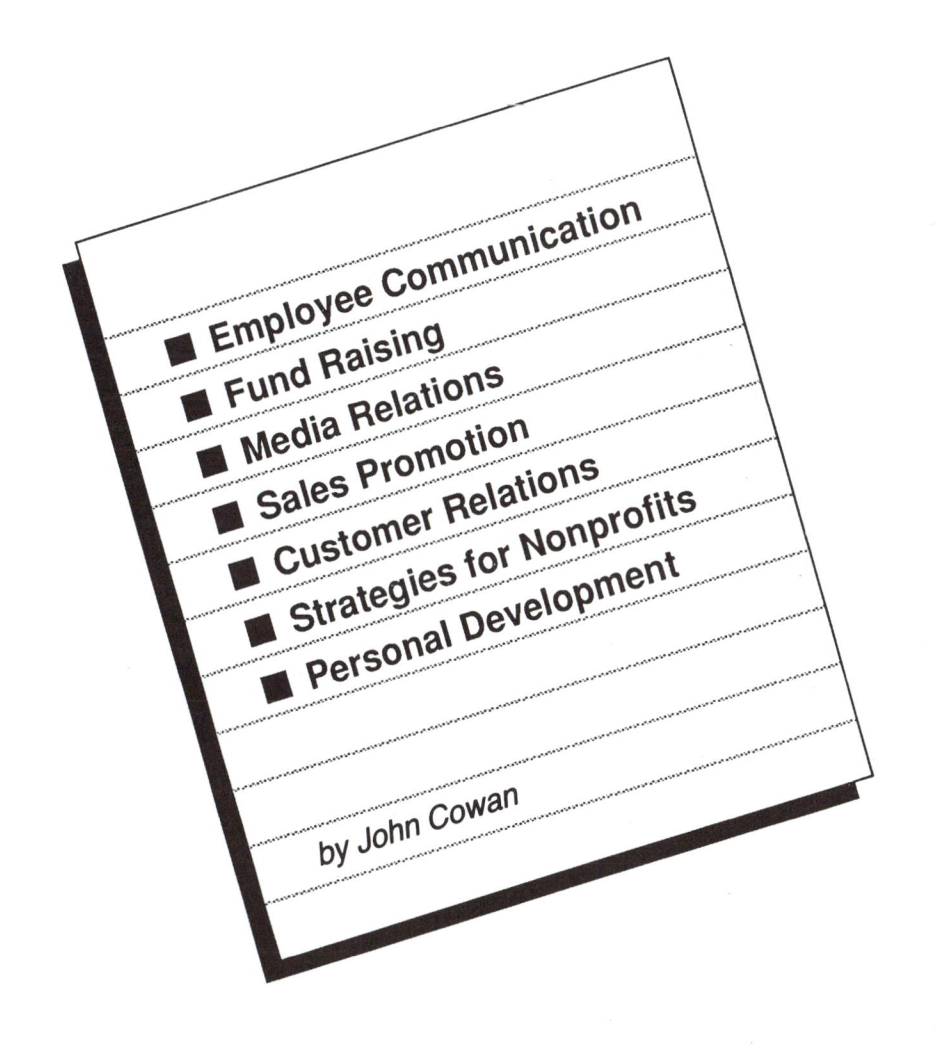

- Employee Communication
- Fund Raising
- Media Relations
- Sales Promotion
- Customer Relations
- Strategies for Nonprofits
- Personal Development

by John Cowan

TABLE OF CONTENTS

Complaints	5
Computers & Faxes	6
Direct mail	11
Handbooks	15
Letters & memos	16
Media relations	22
Meetings	27
News releases	33
Nonprofits	39
Personal relations	41
Photographs — taking	50
Photographs — using	52
Printing mechanics	54
Publishing	61
Speeches & presentations	63
Suppliers	72
Telephone use	74
Time management	80
Tips from readers	89
Video & radio	94
Writing techniques	96

Lawrence Ragan Communications, Inc. publishes the Ragan Report, Speechwriter's Newsletter, Editor's Workshop Newsletter, The Corporate Annual Report Newsletter, Curriculum Review, and The Working Communicator. Please write or call for information about any of these newsletters, or about the 1,000 skills-building workshops that Ragan Communications offers each year.

Lawrence Ragan Communications, Inc.
212 W. Superior Street
Chicago, IL 60610
312-335-0037

COMPLAINTS

In the real world, things don't always go smoothly. Here are some thoughts about handling written complaints from your publics, and also how to phrase your thoughts when the time comes that *you* want to complain.

(*Telephone* complaints are dealt with in the section "Telephone Use.")

Complaints: handle with care

If someone has a grievance with you, remember: No one cares *why* you messed up or what the internal problems of your organization are. All they want to know is this: *What are you going to do about it?*

For example: If you're an editor for an organizational publication and you print faulty information about someone and that person complains, don't go into long, lengthy detail about *why* it happened. Be specific and say, "I'm sorry. Next issue we'll tell all readers — on the front page — of our error."

(*Business Writing Quick & Easy*, by Laura Brill; American Management Association; $7.95)

Resolve complaints

Customer complaints aren't necessarily bad news — as long as they're acted on. One bank in central Florida did some follow-up on customers who had written with specific complaints in the previous year.

Findings: Those whose complaints were resolved demonstrated more loyalty to the bank than those customers who had never complained at all!

(*The American Banker*)

Keep the language of bills soft and gentle

Don't offend customers by writing bills in harsh language. Remember, if they bought from you once, you must work to keep them coming back. *So don't write*: "We have not received last month's payment. If we do not hear from you by May 1, we will close your account." *Instead, write*: "Our records indicate that last month's payment has not been received. Have we made a mistake? If so, please call 555-1234." This is one time the passive voice is acceptable.

(*Nation's Business*, 1615 H Street, N.W., Washington, D.C. 20062)

Get your complaint letters answered

To receive quick action on a complaint letter, send it by certified mail. Why? It gives proof that the letter was received and it tells the recipient that you mean business. When you write the complaint letter, make sure to keep it brief and specific. A single page will do for most grievances.

(*Getting What You Deserve*, Stephen Newmen and Nancy Kramer)

Four pointers for writing a complaint letter

Cheryl Reimold in *How To Write A Million Dollar Memo*, gives four ideas to remember when writing a complaint letter:
- **Don't trade curses and insults**, it defeats your purpose. *Remember*: When you're writing a complaint letter, you want to get a problem solved.
- **Don't write your letter while angry.** "Letters written in anger obscure the subject of the complaints," says Reimold. "The writer is so busy heaping up abuse and the reader so fuming with resentments that the subject itself gets lost."
- **Don't make empty threats.** You'll be the one who looks ridiculous when you can't carry them out.
- **Remember that sarcasm stings.** As Jonathan Swift said: "Whoever is out of patience is out of possession of his soul. Men must not turn into bees who kill themselves in stinging others."

(*How To Write A Million Dollar Memo* by Cheryl Reimold, The Bantam Doubleday Dell Publishing Group; 128 pp; $3.50)

COMPUTERS & FAXES

Today's communicator can't get by with a simple typewriter; at least, most of us can't. The computer has enriched but complicated our lives, and faxes have been catching on even faster than the computer did. Here are some suggestions about getting the most from this electronic gear.

Computer can intrude during phone interviews

For phone interviews, your computer can greatly increase your speed and accuracy in taking notes, but the sound of fingers tapping on the keyboard can distract or intimidate the person you're questioning. If you can't punch the keys softly, use a pen and paper until the interview gets going, and then ask permission to take notes with your computer. This gentle transition allows your subject to get comfortable talking to you without letting your computer intrude on the interview.

Always write with blue pencil

When proofreading the final copy of your newsletter, edit in blue pencil. *Why*? If the computer breaks down you'll be able to work from that copy, and the blue marks won't be captured in the printing photos.

(Steve Moss, *The Record*, St. John's Univ., Collegeville, MN 56321)

Protect your computer from viruses

No one these days needs to be warned about computer "viruses." They seem to be popping up everywhere, causing much damage. To insure that a virus doesn't hit your computer, take these precautions.

☐ Make sure all critical files and programs are regularly backed up. Keep at least three generations of backups to increase chances of "uninfected" data recovery.

☐ Use software that comes only from trusted sources. Don't use unauthorized copies of software.

☐ Do not run freeware, shareware or software that comes from public bulletin boards. Software not approved or owned by the company must not be retained on company premises.

☐ Use "write protect" tabs on all diskettes you do not want written to, either accidentally or by a virus.

☐ Physically lock your computer and floppy disks when not in use.

(*Focus*, 100 Lackawanna Ave., Parsippany, N.J. 07084)

Tips for office computerization

Computerizing your office won't be trouble-free, but you can avoid some of the potential problems by paying attention to these tips from Peter Hubley, of Business Services Development Corporation:

■ *Proceed slowly.* Don't jam the new system down people's throats. Make a list of what needs to be computerized and stick to it, one area at a time.

■ *Go easy at first.* Master word processing before trying to learn desktop publishing. Start with packaged programs like LOTUS before getting customized software. And keep all operations as simple as possible.

■ *Know the area you're computerizing.* You'd better be able to explain in written detail how a job is done before trying to have it computerized. If not, put someone with the appropriate experience in charge of that area.

■ *Don't computerize everything.* Unless the computer will really save the department time and money, or improve customer relations, don't install it. Having a computer shouldn't be an end in itself.

■ *Watch office morale.* The new system should work for your staff, not the other way around. If your people begin to resent the computer, pay attention to *them*. Without their effort and support, the new computer will never turn into the efficient tool it's supposed to be.

(*Hotline*, Newsletter Association, 1401 Wilson Blvd., Suite 403, Arlington, VA 22209)

Rescue erased files with utility programs

Have you ever accidentally erased a file you really wanted to keep? A utility program can rescue you from that and many other kinds of computer disasters. Utility programs aren't new — they've been around since 1982 — but the most recent releases are more powerful and easier to use. Consider getting a utility software package for your system *before* you delete that report that you spent four weeks working on.

(*Time Talk*, 1590 Woodlake Dr., Suite 111, Chesterfield, MO 63017)

Advertise on a FAX machine

If your company uses a facsimile machine, have your designer lay out a crisp, professional looking FAX cover sheet with a couple of lines of promotional or sales copy and perhaps a simple line illustration (in addition to your company's name, address, fax number, voice number and spaces for the recipient's name, recipient's fax number, number of sheets and comments).

(Queen Parker, 340 W. 108th Place, Chicago, IL 60628)

What to look for in a new laser printer

All laser printers are not created equal. Michael Kleper, author of *The Illustrated Handbook of Desktop Publishing and Typesetting*, asks questions like these when looking at a printer:

Speed. How many pages per minute can the machine produce? Is that slower or faster than other models?

Life expectancy. How long will the printer last? What's the industry average?

PDL. Does the printer have any page languages? If so, which ones?

Sheet size. What is the largest page size that the machine can process? How many alternative sizes are available?

Memory. How much RAM does the printer have?

Fonts. Are fonts resident in ROM? Are font cartridges necessary? Can fonts be downloaded? How many type styles can you use simultaneously? What is the available range of point sizes?

Supplies? How much will paper, toner cartridges, and other consumables cost?

Upgrades. Can the printer be given more RAM, ROM, or an additional/replacement controller?

Software support. Will popular software support use of this brand and model?

(*Newsletter on Newsletters*, 44 W. Market St., Rhinebeck, NY 12572)

Hog wild isn't the way to go

Your new desktop publishing investment may include the ability to use several, perhaps dozens of different typestyles. Resist the temptation to combine several in one publication. Your material will actually be much more readable if you use *one* suitable typestyle, with a mixture of bold, italic, and different type sizes serving to maintain reader interest.

(Ray Dorn, Design consultant, 1013 S. Ahrens, Lombard, IL 60148)

Mail important items electronically

Reserve electronic mail for your most important or timely communiques. Sometimes it is more economical to mail such items electronically. When using electronic mail:
- Change your password periodically.
- Don't overtax your system.
- Delete old messages regularly.

(Jean Burke Hoppe, writing in *Measure*, Hewlett Packard, P.O. Box 10301, Palo Alto, CA 94303)

Increase your speed on the computer

If you have a Macintosh, you don't have to reach into the Editing or Format menus for many functions. There's a much simpler way that's often overlooked.

Command/Shift/>, for example, makes words and letters larger by increments; Command/Shift/< makes them smaller.

Command/Shift/h gives you ALL CAPS; Command/Shift/i gives you *italics*; Command/Shift/u underlines. Hitting the key a second time undoes your changes.

Keep computer files neat

If you work with desktop publishing, use folders for your files. The more files you have on your desk the longer it takes to display the contents. If you group files into folders, your computer will start up faster. **Remember:** Always delete files as soon as you no longer need them. They take up disk space and slow down your system.

(*Desktop Publishing*, Pioneer Hi-Bred International, Inc., 6800 Pioneer Parkway, Johnson, IA 50131)

Speed up orders: include FAX number

If other businesses are the target of your sales efforts, include your FAX number in all your advertising. Your customers will find that sending a purchase order by FAX is quicker and less subject to error than making the arrangements by phone.

(*Success*)

Desktop dilemmas? Simplify with stylesheet

Many people with very limited graphics background have become responsible for the design of everything from a company newsletter to an entire magazine. The best assurance of a consistent readable document is to keep the design simple and to keep a stylesheet for each publication.

Deborah J. Smyth, director of Administrative Services at Fairfax County schools has developed a simple stylesheet.

Page margins
Top _____
Bottom _____
Sides _____

Format
Number of pages _____
Page size _____

Text
Number of columns _____
Column width _____
Type style _____
Type size _____
Space between lines _____
Space between graphs _____

Headlines
Style _____
Size _____
☐ Downstyle
☐ Initial caps

Credit lines/bylines
Type style _____
Type size _____
☐ Top
☐ Bottom
☐ Centered

Captions
Type style _____
Type size _____

Masthead
Type style _____
Type size _____
Information included _____

DIRECT MAIL

Despite the ever-mounting costs of postage, direct mail has become an important tool of the communicator's trade. Helpful tips here can make your direct mail more productive.

Use the most effective words to sell ideas

A Yale University study found that these are the eleven most effective words you can use today:

Discover ... ease ... guarantee ... health ... love ... money ... new ... proven ... results ... save ... you.

These words have the strongest chance of persuading readers, because readers understand them more easily than any other words in the vocabulary. Managers who need to sell or just to explain should rely on the communication power of these words.

Successful direct-mail copywriting

Don Hauptman has had 13 years of copywriting experience. Here are five of his principles and techniques for writing direct-mail materials:

■ *Start with the prospect instead of the product.* Avoid superlatives and brag-and-boast language. Wherever possible, incorporate anecdotes, testimonials, success stories, and other believable elements of human interest.

■ *Do research.* Interview customers, ask questions, listen carefully. Hauptman's favorite question is "What are your [the prospect's] greatest problems, needs, and concerns right now?" At least half the time he spends on an assignment is pure research — before attacking the blank page or computer screen.

■ *Use specifics to add power and credibility.* Use precise, documented figures and facts in advertising. Cite data or opinions from outside, impartial sources. A lot of copy is anemic and ineffective because it's superficial, vague, and unspecific. Concrete statements and detail supply the ring of truth. But to find this kind of material, you've often got to dig for it.

■ *Don't try to change behavior.* It's time-consuming, expensive, and often futile. It's usually wise to capitalize on existing motivations. In other words, preach to the converted. Unless you have an unlimited budget, avoid products and services that require the buyer to be educated or radically transformed.

■ *Be a "creative plagiarist."* You can learn by studying the work of others. But don't imitate; emulate or re-create. When you see an idea you admire, try to identify the principles behind it, then apply those principles in a fresh, original way to your own work.

State benefits simply, easily

Sure, you believe in your product or service. It's your livelihood. But don't make the mistake of assuming that its benefits are as obvious to others. Your press release, sales pitch or trade show exhibit is likely to fall flat when your target has to work to find the benefit. A few simply-stated, easily remembered benefit statements placed right up front will create a receptive audience for all that follows.

(*INC*. Magazine)

Long letters are worth money

Don't write a short business-to-business sales letter just because you figure people don't have time to read a longer letter. Statistics show that long outpulls short in every type of business and at every age and educational level. Three to four pages would not be too long. Direct mail guru Rene Gnam advises, "Write it as long as it has to be." The idea is that you have to state a problem and a solution, and people subconsciously feel that a problem that can be solved in one page isn't worth a chunk of their money.

Target your marketing with database directory

The number of databases has increased from 300 to 3,000 in 10 years. Gale Research has published a directory, *Computer Readable Databases: A Directory and Data Sourcebook*, that can help you find the databases most appropriate to your marketing objectives. To order the *Directory*, or have a database listed in it, write *Directory*, Computer Readable Databases, Gale Research Co., Book Tower, Detroit, MI 48226; (313) 961-2242.

Adjust margins for some letters

When you write a business letter, vary the margins according to the length of the letter. This will make the letter easier to read.

A short letter (body less than 100 words) about 4 inches wide.
Set margins at 35 and 75.

Average letter (body 100-200 words) about 5 inches wide.
Set margins at 30 and 80.

A long letter (body 200+ words) about 6 inches wide.
Set margins at 25 and 85.

(*Better Letters*, by Jan Venolia, Ten Speed Press, P.O. Box 7123, Berkeley, CA 94707)

Write better sales letters

Author Mary Jean Parson offers the following advice on writing stronger copy for sales letters in her new book, *Managing the 1-Person Business*. Letters should:
1. **Seize** the reader's attention quickly by stating the benefit in the very first sentence.
2. **Establish** a bond of friendly mutual self-interest.
3. **Tell** positively and without apology how the product or service can help the reader.
4. **Refer** to an enclosed brochure or reply form that describes the offer in more detail.
5. **Push** for immediate action in an order or sales inquiry.

(*Association Trends*, 4948 St. Elmo Ave., Bethesda, MD 20814)

Get rid of that unsightly post office box

If you'd like your mail delivered to a post office box, but don't like the inconvenience or the image, you have an alternative; a commercial mail receiving agency.

Many businesses are finding that these agencies offer several advantages over post offices:
- Mail receiving agencies offer a prestigious street address, which the post office doesn't do, and the customer can use the post office box number as a suite or room number.
- Boxes are available immediately. At some post offices you have to wait up to six months.
- Many agencies offer 24-hour access to the mail or forward mail to your actual address.
- Agencies can sign for packages. The U.S. Post Office cannot.
- Agencies can arrange pickups from UPS and other alternative mail carriers.

(Adapted from a news segment from *ABC News*.)

One way to get repeat business

If a customer has left you for some reason, try to get him or her back by writing a letter. Many of your past customers, approached in a warm enthusiastic letter, will come back. *Why?* Because it's nice to be wanted.

☐ Tell your old customers you'd be glad to have them back. Your letter should convey enthusiasm, and seem as if you are renewing ties with an old friend.

☐ Let customers know that you plan to keep in touch with them. Provide your direct number so they can reach you personally.

☐ Send along information about products and services you provide.

(*Money Making Marketing* by Dr. Jeffrey Lant, 50 Follen St., Cambridge, MA 02138)

The magic word is FREE
The easiest way to command attention is to tell people they'll get something free. Here's an example:
   If you have a special promotion on a $20 product, you could advertise it these three ways:
- ☐ Buy two, get 50% off.
- ☐ Buy one for $19.99, get the second for a penny.
- ☐ Buy one, get one FREE.

All three offers are the same, but the last sounds like a more attractive deal and will most likely achieve a better response.

Three ways to make letters more personal
1. **In a one-page letter**, use the reader's name only once in addition to the inside address and salutation.
2. **Use the name in a crucial spot** — to direct your reader's attention to a key point. Example: *Bill, as you'll notice on the spec sheet, our model D15 meets your exact specifications.*
3. **If you haven't used the name elsewhere** in the letter, use it at the end — as long as it sounds natural.

Increase your direct-mail response
Next time you print a promotional brochure, include more than one order form in the brochure. Rene Gnam, direct-mail marketing consultant, says that when he added another order form to his brochure, response improved dramatically.
   Editor's note: For a FREE newsletter by Rene Gnam with direct-mail marketing tips, write: Rene Gnam Consultation Corp., Response Ranch, 1 Response Rd., Box 3877, Holiday, FL 34690-3877.

Rules for organizing a persuasive letter
If you're looking for a way to judge the persuasiveness of your business correspondence, here are five principles to guide you.

■ Don't try to con your reader. State your request clearly and immediately.

■ Show why the action desired is in the reader's or the company's best interest. But don't sound like a huckster.

■ Convince the reader (by use of meaningful and honest evidence) that what you want is reasonable.

■ Specify how, when and where the desired action should be taken.

■ Make the action required as simple as possible. ("Just initial a copy of this letter, send it back to me, and I'll place the order.")

(*What Do You Mean I Can't Write?* by John S. Fielden and Ronald E. Dulek)

Fear outpulls greed by two to one

One of the many questions that plague direct-mail marketers is what tactic to use when writing copy. Should they play on their prospects' fears? For example, should the underlying tone be: "If you don't buy this product you will fail at your job?" Or should direct-mail marketers play on feelings of greed: "If you buy this product you will make more money?"

Magna Publications Inc. confronted this problem recently. The marketers did a test on two promotions, one emphasizing fear, the other greed. And fear outpulled greed by two to one.

(The Newsletter on Newsletters, 44 West Market St., P.O. Box 311, Rhinebeck, NY 12572)

HANDBOOKS

The employee handbook has become just about indispensable, especially in large organizations. Here are some cautionary features you may not have considered.

The employee's handbook: Beware!

Beware of information casually inserted in employee handbooks. Employee communications specialist Ron Wohl, president of In Plain English, reminds us that employee benefit information takes on a life of its own — falling into the hands of courts, lawyers, insurance companies and other parties with no company loyalty and a shot at some of your company's funds. Also, if an insurance company won't pay and your manual said you'd be covered for the item, the courts may throw it back into your lap. The solution? Hire a professional manual writer to write your manual. "The greatest mistake," says Wohl, "is to opt for a cheap writer. An editor is not necessarily a writer. An English major is not necessarily a writer. A PR professional is not necessarily a writer. A manual writer writes manuals all the time."

Talk can beat writing

An example: the employee handbook. Given to new employees, the handbook is often symbolic communication. It is there. It comforts everybody to know that the rules are explained and the health plan described.

Like a telephone book, it is a reference source that can be used when needed.

But often it isn't. When employees want to know how much their insurance will pay for three days in the hospital, they'll go to the people who have the answers and ask them. Almost certainly they will not go to the handbook.

The moral: Some communication efforts demand oral explanations. Writing reinforces the explanation and gives it authority.

(Robert Friedman, *TWC* editor)

Avoid legal battles over employee handbooks

When producing an employee handbook, you can avoid future legal troubles by clearly stating in the introduction that the handbook only *summarizes* the formal rules, policies, and contracts of the company — it doesn't supersede them, and doesn't, by itself, create a contract between employees and the company. Don't let the president or any other representative of the company sign the introduction, either; some courts treat a signed introduction as a contractual obligation.

(*Communication for Motivation*, Wyatt Company, (312) 704-0600)

LETTERS & MEMOS

No way they can be avoided. Written communications — up, down, and across — are woven into the fabric of American enterprise. These helpful hints can make your letters and memos more effective.

A conversational tone is best

Whether you're writing to subordinates, peers, or higher-ups, a conversational tone will draw people to your point of view. For example:

Formal: *I would suggest that you remit the balance in full within 10 days of receipt of this notice.*
Conversational: *Please send us a check for the balance of the payment by 3/15.*
Formal: *Please be advised that we are processing your claims for monthly benefits.*
Conversational:*We're processing your claims for monthly benefits.*

By writing this way, you'll be seen as a person, not a bureaucrat who doesn't understand the lives of others.

Advertising techniques bring success to memos

Don't be afraid to use the techniques of advertising in your business communications. Even the most routine memos can benefit:

- Break up the size of type blocks. For instance, move in the margins of a particularly important paragraph two or more inches on both sides.
- Use boldfaced, action-oriented headlines and subheads.
- Underline key phrases.
- Use bulleted lists rather than lines of narrative.
- Be aggressive in your use of white space. For instance, a memo of one or two paragraphs typically occupies the top few lines of the page. If you center those lines in the middle of the page, and surround it dramatically by white space, you will draw your readers into the story.

16 • Techniques for Communicators

Avoid ending letters with cliches

Do you end your letters with a formulaic tag line that's devoid of meaning?
☐ **A typical ending:** "Please feel free to contact me if you have any questions." Instead, end letters by spelling out the next steps you expect.
☐ **Your closing lines could be:** *I'll look for your response in the next few days; I'll be glad to answer any questions; I'll call you to discuss further.*

Be concise when writing

Wordy writing is weak writing. To write more powerfully, follow these rules:

1. Remove unnecessary modifiers.
   We *absolutely* guarantee all our products.
   Her contribution was *very* crucial to our success.
2. Don't identify places, books, or objects that are self-evident.
   Not: He is from the city of Houston.
   But: He is from Houston.
3. Avoid beginning your sentences with empty words such as *frankly, essentially,* and *basically.*
4. Whenever possible, remove phrases such as *at the rate of* and *in the time of.*
   Not: He types at the rate of 55 wpm.
   But: He types 55 wpm.
5. Avoid the expression *serve as a*. Rephrase the sentence or try substituting *is* or *are*.
   Not: She serves as our proofreader.
   But: She is our proofreader.
6. Avoid the phrase *the reason is because*. You can often trim it down to *because* by rewording the sentence.
   Not: The reason he finishes early is because he is organized.
   But: He finishes early because he is organized.

(*Style, Darn Ya, Style,* F&W Publications, and cited in *Writer's Digest,* 1507 Dana Ave., Cincinnati, OH 45207)

That's a lot of money!

If you write a memo a week, it's costing your company. Routine documents are *rewritten* 4.2 times *within* an organization, and *then* are sent to their intended audience, a recent survey shows.

Fifty-four minutes are spent planning, composing and editing the average memo or letter. Therefore, if an employee earns $35,000 a year ($17.50 an hour), the 54 minutes it takes to write a memo costs the company $15.75. If he or she rewrites the memo 4.2 times, that's $81.90. If one memo a week is written, his communication is costing $4,258.60 a year.

(*Personnel Journal,* 245 Fischer Ave., B-2, Costa Mesa, CA 92626)

In reports, give plenty of detail

Can't decide if your boss is more interested in detail or brevity? The editors of *Executive Productivity* suggest that you make it a habit of giving him or her both. Always begin a lengthy report with a paragraph (no more!) containing an analysis and recommendation, if appropriate. Don't be afraid to oversimplify, as long as you dwell on the nuances in the meat of the report.

Edit out the excess

Never rush a letter into the mail while it's still hot. Let it cool. Go work on something else for a while, then come back to edit. As one goal of your editing session, you'll want to root out wordiness. These three editing tips will help you find excess words — and eradicate them:

1. **Underline "be," "being," "been."**
   Wordy: Orders are *being processed* as soon as they are received.
   Concise: We're processing orders as soon as we receive them.
2. **Underline infinitives.** Too many infinitive phrases make a wordy sentence.
   Wordy: We are going *to conduct* a poll *to determine* who buys our product.
   Concise: We will conduct a poll to determine who buys our product.
3. **Underline word forms ending in "ion"** and omit as many as possible.
   Wordy: The *communications* trainers in your *institution* should have *information* on a new *communications organization*.
   Concise: Your communications trainers should know about a new professional organization.

Be positive — but not until end

Negative letters almost always contain an opening "buffer" section, a bit of cheeriness meant to soften the blow that follows. According to the *Journal of Business Communication*, however, buffers have just the opposite effect on people who see them frequently (such as job seekers), and the ill will the writer is trying to avoid is instead intensified. *Suggestion*: Skip the buffer, and lead with the bad news. If you have something positive to say, close with it. You'll project sincerity, and the recipient will appreciate your honesty.

Handwriting gets attention

A handwritten note in the margin of your typewritten letter gets attention. Never hesitate to pencil in a note (with a pen) if you want to add to something already in your typewritten version.

Do the same when you write a sales letter. The handwritten note calling attention to a special offer, a time deadline, a special premium gets the attention.

Editors, you can use this technique, too, when you don't have time to illustrate or photograph a story. Try using your own handwriting to add drama.

Start letters off right

To get your letters off to a good start, follow these guidelines:

☐ **Limit your first sentence to 17 words.** If the sentence is longer than 17 words (or 20 words at most), edit. You want a short, concise opening sentence.

☐ **Make your opening words strong and clear.** You'll get into trouble right off the bat if you start out with the wrong word. Red flags should pop up if you use words in any of these three groups:
   A. Pronouns "I" and "This". "I" is OK anywhere else — but *not* the first word of the first sentence. The most basic rule of business writing is "put the reader first." Instead of beginning your memo to the personnel director, "I would like to suggest trying flextime hours this summer," try saying this: "Would you consider using flextime hours this summer?"
   "This" is all right as the first word of the first sentence *only when you refer to time*: "This week. . ." Otherwise, it usually precedes trite and wordy openings such as "This is in reference to your August 15 letter."
   B. Prepositions. When you begin sentences with prepositions, the sentence is sure to start slowly: "In an effort to provide employees with more flexibility this summer, I would like to suggest that we try flextime." Instead, put the prepositional phrase at the end of the sentence: "Let's try flextime hours to give employees more flexibility this summer."
   C. Participles. Participles are those "ing" words such as "referring," "responding," "regarding." If you begin with participles, you'll get off to a slow and wordy start: "According to our phone conversation yesterday, I think we should try flextime scheduling this summer."

☐ **Limit your introductory paragraph to three sentences.** That way you won't write run-on introductions. If possible, use one-sentence introductory paragraphs: *Let's try flextime hours this summer.*

Three ways to end a memo

• **The signpost ending.** If you want action, the end of the memo is the place to ask for it. "Thank you for considering this proposal. I look forward to discussing its possible applications in your lab work when we meet March 1."
• **The emphatic ending.** Leave the reader with one important idea. "Devoting extra support to this project now may save us more than $3,000 in the next three years."
• **The provocative ending.** Don't save important information for the end. That would be bad organization and might annoy the reader. But the right information, building on what already has been said, also leads to action: "So far, 595 people from 12 companies in four major industries have taken this seminar. Come and find out what was worth more than a day's work to all of them!"
   End your memo, in other words, with a bang, not a whimper.

(Cheryl Remold, author of *How to Write a Million-Dollar Memo*, writing in *Executive Female*, 1041 Third Ave., New York, NY 10021)

How to address a woman

A host of problems confront the person addressing a woman. Should you use Mrs. or Ms., a married woman's first name or her husband's? And what about divorcees or widows? The best guide is what the woman herself prefers ... but if you don't know, use these guidelines:

- Use Ms. if marital status is unknown.
- In business, use a married woman's first name (Mrs. Evelyn Stone); socially, the custom has been to use her husband's first name (Mrs. Stephen Stone). However, customs change, and the choice of names is now more a matter of personal preference than it was in the past.
- For a widowed or divorced woman, use her first name and married name, unless she has chosen to return to her maiden name. In general, use Mrs. when addressing married, widowed, or divorced women, unless you know that Ms. is preferred.

(Jan Venolia, *Better Letters*, Periwinkle Press, P.O. Box 7123, Berkeley, CA 94707)

The first rule of letter writing: 'Be polite'

So advises Amnesty International, whose letter-writing campaigns last for years and involve human lives.

But their basic advice is useful to any business person: "The aim is to convince rather than debate. Forgo anger, criticism, and sarcasm; strive to be reasonable and persuasive."

Other advice for letter writers from Amnesty International:

- Visualize your correspondent.
- Develop the habit of letter writing.
- Try to limit your letters to one page.
- Give immediate explanation of why you're writing — somewhere in the first paragraph.
- Never begin with something your reader already knows. For example: "You wrote to us on April 3 to ask for. . . ."
- Never baffle your reader with jargon. Try to use normal, everyday language. The more personal, the better.
- When you end the letter, don't say: "I'm looking forward to meeting you." It's a cliche and, because it's always used, no one believes it. Try instead something like: "It will be fun when we get together." Use your imagination.
- Purchase stamps in rolls so you can get the letter in the mail without delay.
- Once you send the letter, don't agonize over it.

(Adapted in part from *Salt*, 205 W. Monroe St., Chicago, IL 60606)

Too many requests? Refuse them carefully

We offer the following five rules to help you out of a sticky situationHow to refuse a request firmly, while leaving the reader with a good feeling:
1. Begin with a neutral comment.
2. Give reasons for the refusal.
3. State the refusal directly unless it can be easily inferred.
4. Offer an alternative when possible.
5. End on a positive note. Don't use cliches; don't restate the refusal; don't apologize.

Here's an example of a letter that refuses a request but maintains good will:

Dear Mr. Grace:
    I received your letter of May 10 telling of your class's participation in the Children's Hospital benefit. It is heart-warming to see teenagers such as yourself becoming involved in community service.
    Because of the danger of possible injury, only authorized personnel are allowed on the grounds of the Delco Power Station; therefore, we would not be able to allow students to conduct a sales campaign on the premises. However, we *would* like to help you, so we are enclosing a check for $25 as a donation.
    Good luck with your sales campaign to benefit the hospital.
                              Sincerely,
                              John H. Doogood

One-second workshop

Keep your memos personal: Count 100 words in a random memo. If there aren't 15 personal words — I, me, you, we, they, etc. — in those hundred, your memos are probably ineffective because they are dry and abstract.

(*202 Time-saving Tips for the Business Writer,* Ragan Communications, 212 W. Superior Street, Chicago, IL 60610)

Get action from your memos

Before readers can respond to your memos, they have to read the memos.
    How can you make sure that your readers don't automatically put correspondence from you at the bottom of the pile? Let your reader know that you don't take more time than needed to communicate an idea.

☐ Use an informative subject line.

☐ Highlight your main point at the start of the memo.

☐ Clearly state what kind of response you need from the reader.

    Busy people don't like to spend five minutes reading a memo that has one minute's worth of ideas. If you come straight to the point, your reader will reward you by paying attention to what you say.

MEDIA RELATIONS

Don't panic. You (or your boss, or your boss's boss) may be visited by a reporter at any moment. But if you've done your homework, there's nothing to fear. Not much, anyway.

To deal with reporters, recognize their priorities

The secret of successful media relations may lie in recognizing that reporters have their own priorities. Dean Rotbart, editor of *The Journalist and Financial Reporting*, ranks reporters' priorities in this order:

Number one: the reporter. Journalists put themselves first when working on a story, Rotbart says. They are motivated by money, public recognition, and ego gratification, and not by the desire to perform public service.

The editor. As with everyone else, a reporter's boss has more influence than anyone in how a job is done.

Sources. A reporter needs well-placed, trustworthy sources of information. Vital for gathering and checking facts, a good source helps shape the reporter's opinions, and keeps the reporter "on the straight and narrow," in Rotbart's words.

Rival journalists. Increasingly tight competition in the news business is making news judgment a tool for scoring victories over other newspapers, not a question of informing readers. And speaking of readers...

The audience. No matter that journalists say they place the reader first, says Rotbart, "It isn't true."

Last — your company. Most journalists don't respect or trust business executives. According to one survey, three-quarters believe senior managers would lie to them if they thought they could get away with it. Rotbart compares reporters to doctors: "If it wasn't for disease, doctors would be out of business, but they have very little loyalty to the disease."

Overly cynical? Perhaps. But Rotbart's list reminds us that reporters have their own needs, priorities, and agendas. Recognize what they're after, and you can work together to satisfy the needs of both your company and the reporters covering you.

Don't let the press intimidate you

Here's advice from Herb Schmertz, former public relations executive with Mobil Oil Co.: "Often, when reporters approach you for an interview, they will imply that you have no real choice in the matter. They may say or suggest that if you don't cooperate, you'll be violating some unwritten law, or that your non-cooperation will make you look bad. Don't fall for any of this. Always talk to the press because you want to, or because it will be good for you or your institution. But never do so because you have to."

(*Good-Bye to the Low Profile* by Herb Schmertz, Little, Brown and Co., Boston; $16.95)

Recognize reporters' probe questions

A probe question gives you the chance to make sure the reporter understands what you've said and the opportunity to elaborate further on the subject. Here are some types of probe questions to listen for and recognize:
- **Clarification:** "What do you mean?" Could you rephrase that?"
- **Justification:** "What's your reasoning for that statement?" "What would someone opposing you say to that?"
- **Refocus:** "How would you relate that to ..." "How does your competition's response influence your position?"
- **Prompting:** "If you say x, you must mean this." "Here's one possible response to that issue...."
- **Redirecting the question** (if another person is present): "Ms. Smith, do you agree?" "How would you respond to that, Mr. Jones?"

(Georgeson & Company, Wall Street Plaza, New York, NY 10005)

Know these guidelines for talking to the media

To enhance your organization's public image, follow these interview guidelines:

☐ Honesty is the best policy. Don't be afraid to admit a mistake. Doing so increases your credibility with both the reporter and the story's readers — an audience which may include your own employees and stockholders.

☐ Avoid defensiveness and evasion. A pleasant, helpful response to all queries builds the "we have nothing to hide" image.

☐ Interviews are opportunities, not chores. Don't pass them off to lower-level staff who may not know as much about the company and its projects. Regard an interview as your chance to educate the public about your company.

☐ Don't expect interviewers to be experts. They often don't have time to thoroughly research every aspect of your operations. Take the risk of explaining what they may already know, rather than confusing them with more information than they can handle.

☐ Prepare for an interview as carefully as you would for a speech or presentation. Have some short quotes ready ahead of time to sum up past activities, clarify present plans, and project future goals.

☐ Be sensitive to the interviewer's deadline pressures. Be ready to direct him or her to alternative sources of information if more data are needed in a hurry.

☐ Think about the people who will read the story. They need reliable facts, not empty phrases. Help the audience, and the reporter, by providing relevant, accurate information.

☐ Don't cry wolf to get attention. Contact the news media when something important actually takes place, not just when you want publicity.

(*pr reporter*, No. 256, as cited in *Communicating Title III*, Chemical Manufacturers Association, 2501 M Street NW, Washington, DC 20037)

Twelve points to review before the interview

Director of Media Relations for Ketchum PR, Jonathan M. Schenker, offers the following:

1. Remember you are a guest and the authority on your topic.
2. Anticipate contrary points of view.
3. Plan your main points and make them early in your interview.
4. Watch the TV show, listen to the radio program, or read the paper in which you will appear.
5. Reply positively to negative questions.
6. Be brief.
7. If you don't understand a question, ask for clarification.
8. Don't panic if you must pause to gather your thoughts.
9. If an untruth is made, refute it immediately.
10. Don't speak over the heads of your audience. They are not in your business or familiar with your idioms.
11. Be vigorous. Every interview is a performance. If you are bored, it will be obvious.
12. Don't bury your points in statistics.

"The bottom line for every media interview is communication, as the public wants more information about business and the press responds," says Schenker. "That's good for the manager and his or her company. Whether TV or print, the news media offer a tremendous opportunity for a manager to see, discuss, and share his or her thoughts and those of the organization."

A reporter's rules: know them — or else

Here are the commonly accepted interview rules when dealing with reporters:

☐ **On the record:** Everything you say can be used, you can be quoted by name.

☐ **Not for attribution** and **On background:** You can be quoted but not directly identified. You may be described in such phrases as "a top company official" or "an aide close to Congressman Jones."

☐ **On deep background:** Whatever the reporter uses cannot be linked to you at all but must be asserted on the journalist's own authority.

☐ **Off the record:** The material cannot be used in any form except to guide the reporter's thinking. This agreement is sometimes broken if a story becomes public or if the journalist finds other sources who will attest to it.

Remember: If you say to a reporter, "This is off the record," the reporter has to agree to it — or you might be quoted.

(*Winning Them Over*, Prima Publishing and Communications, P.O. Box 1260JR, Rocklin, CA 95677)

Ask questions when you are interviewed

Naturally you want to please reporters when they call for interviews — that's just good publicity — but that doesn't mean you don't have a right to ask the *reporter* some questions.

Ask for the reporter's name and where he or she works (the professional will tell you immediately), and get the phone number in case you have additional information later on.

Is the reporter a staff reporter or freelancer? What magazine or newsletter is he or she writing for? If you know that, you'll get a sense of the story the reporter is trying to write.

Ask when the deadline is. *Why*? If it's soon, you'll probably have to give shorter answers. Try to sum up your answers, and repeat them for clarity.

It's within bounds to ask the reporter to repeat the main points you think you've made.

Don't be fooled by simple-sounding questions. A good reporter is trained to ask "dumb" questions because those are the ones the editor and reader will probably ask.

Use anecdote, analogy, and example in an effort to simplify your answers. Don't try to impress a reporter with your technical knowledge. Don't baffle with jargon.

(Mack Laing, Associate Professor in the Graduate School of Journalism, University of Western Ontario, writing in *Contact*, Natural Sciences and Engineering Research Council of Canada, Ottawa, Canada K1A 1H5)

Off the record: "Don't talk!"

If you talk to reporters, remember that some reporters respect the "off the record" phrase, and some don't. So the best thing to remember, says Roger Ailes, a one-time consultant to President Reagan, is: "The only thing off the record is what you don't say."

(*You Are The Message, Secrets of The Master Communicators* by Roger Ailes, Dow Jones-Irwin)

Be ready for the media's toughest questions

Take ten minutes and write out the answers to what many executives say are the five toughest questions posed by newspapers or radio:
1. What does your company do?
2. What do you do in the company? (So your mother or brother can understand.)
3. Where does your company fit into your industry?
4. What does your company give back to the community?
5. What is your company doing to advance women and minorities?
    To be prepared for an interview, you should be able to answer each of these five questions in 60 to 120 words.

(James Lukaszewski's *Executive Action*)

How to survive when meeting the press

Jack Hilton's *How to Meet the Press — A Survival Guide* tells the executive what to say and how to say it when confronted by the press, print and electronic media. Some of his advice:

Be brief. For television, that's the first rule. Hilton guesses that the interviewed guest on a morning TV news show is permitted to speak 344 words. Asked eight questions, the guest has 43 words and 15 seconds to reply to each.

Be prepared. On national television, no executive should be permitted the luxury of the ad-lib. He points to President Reagan's famous response in the second TV debate to a question about age: "I will not make age an issue in this campaign. I'm not going to exploit for political purposes my opponent's youth and inexperience." Reagan was waiting — and was prepared.

Communicate your message. No law says that you have to answer the question asked of you. Example: A reporter asks Ed Newman to point to the "finest program" in his career. "I can't do that," says Newman. *"But I can tell you what* (our itals) exhilarates me the most about our business. It's the emergencies. . ." The italicized words are what Hilton refers to as "the bridge" — the way the responder leads into what he or she in fact wants to say, instead of replying to whatever is asked.

Speak conversationally. Yes, if you're addressing a political rally of thousands, the occasion calls for declamation. If you're on TV, do your best to think you're speaking to one person just behind the camera.

Be liked. Be yourself. No pretensions, no sarcasm. Remain cool when an interviewer bullies you. If you're liked, you'll win, even if you fail to convey your message.

Dress like a banker. You'll never go wrong with blue, grey, or brown. Black sometimes absorbs too much color. For men, knee-length socks are a must. For men, keep the double-breasted coat buttoned. Wear solids with only one subdued pattern, perhaps in a tie or shirt.

Beware of the A-B dilemma question. It goes like this: "Which country is nuttier to deal with — Syria or Libya?" Or, "Is your company more interested in profits, or the public welfare?" On taking charge of the New York Rangers hockey team, Alan Cohen was asked whether he'd rather win the Stanley Cup or make a profit. When he replied "a profit," he won the nickname, "Bottom Line Cohen."

Jack Hilton's book at first blush is for the limited audience of those who are interviewed on television or radio. But those who work with such people will find it invaluable. And those who want to learn more about practical techniques in the world of communication — and the anecdotes, the sayings, the famous examples — will find it fascinating.

(Dodd Mead & Co., 71 Fifth Ave., New York, NY 10003; $19.95)

Show compassion

When a disaster or crisis occurs in your workplace, try these suggestions from Thomas Hunter, Director of Public Relations for Union Camp Corporation:
1. **Make** key people available immediately.
2. **Get** the whole story out all at once or it will dribble on forever.
3. **Don't** downplay bad news. Show compassion for just how tragic something tragic is.
4. **Be** absolutely accurate about statements.
5. **Tell** the truth. If you made a mistake, say so. Be credible.
6. **Convey** a sense of concern for the victims or people affected. And it must be a true sense of concern.

(*Speechwriter's Newsletter,* 212 W. Superior Street, Chicago, IL 60610)

MEETINGS

If you're called on to organize a meeting, you'll have a thousand details to think about. These tips, many of which aren't likely to appear in any manual you have around, could spare you embarrassment and insure success.

Next time, travel wrinkle-free

When you travel, the fastest, most wrinkle-proof way to pack is to interfold clothing. Flight attendants frequently use this method unknown to most travelers. To interfold clothes, place a garment with its top lying against one edge of the suitcase; the bottom half of the garment hangs out over the side of the suitcase. Lay in the suitcase as many items as you are taking, piling them up with all the ends hanging out (place long items horizontally, short items vertically). After everything is in place, flip the ends up into the suitcase. You will end up with each garment padding another at a crucial fold line.

(*How to Pack Your Suitcase...and Other Travel Tips* , by Chris Evatt, Random House, 400 Hahn Rd., Westminister, MD 21157, cited in *The American School Board Journal*)

Lunch breaks at meetings

If you are conducting a day-long meeting, remember to tell the group these four things as it breaks for lunch;
1. The room where lunch will be held.
2. The precise time when you'll reconvene.
3. Any topics they might discuss over lunch.
4. "Please take your valuables."

(Michael Omahoney, Meeting planner, 220 12th Ave. E., Seattle, WA 98102)

How to spot phony charges

While you're attending a conference, you charge a variety of meals, drinks, etc., to your room. At check out, your bill has a long list of items. *How do you know they're all yours?* **It's easy:** Whenever you sign a bill for a tippable service, add a sum to makethe total end with a 7. **For example:** If your dinner bill is $18.25, add a $2.92 tip so the total is $21.17.

When you get the final bill, scan for any numbers that don't end in 7. If the charge is for room, tax, or telephone, it's OK. If it isn't — you're paying someone else's tab!

(Mon Valley Travel CEO Marc Zelenski, writing in *Dymic Business*, 1400 S. Braddock Ave., Pittsburgh, PA 15218)

Let them know how to dress for conferences

Conference attenders are often confused as to what they should wear, because meeting planners fail in providing specific suggestions. Some guidelines:

- In general, the more business, the more business-like the dress should be. But every meeting will have reservations, amplifications, and qualifications to that rule.

- Planners should be specific about weather. Don't say "warm," but say "warm and dry" or "warm and very humid."

- The location means a lot. New York is more formal than Los Angeles. One conference attender says she wears pastels in the South but is partial to black in northern California.

- Built into the conference should be enough time for people to change clothes. The conference-ending ball shoud not take place exactly after the tennis match.

- Speakers shoud be counseled as to the style of dress that may be appropriate to a corporate culture.

- Give more information rather than less when advising attenders what to wear. "Formal" may not mean the same thing to everybody. Recent buzz words like "casually elegant" are confusing. One conference attender says, that "casually elegant" reminds him of Miami Vice and $300 T-shirts.

(*Successful Meetings*, $5 a copy, Bill Communications, Inc., 633 Third Ave., New York NY 10017)

Take care when arranging chairs

If you conduct a meeting between two opposing groups, be sure to intermix people around the meeting table. If opposing groups sit on different sides, you're setting up what amounts to "battle lines" — and nothing more than bickering and arguing will take place.

(Adapted in part form *How To Run Better Business Meetings* by the 3M Meeting Management Team, McGraw-Hill Book Co.; hardcover, $18.95.)

28 • Techniques for Communicators

Executives won't forget you

If you or your company hosts visitors from out of town, make the visits as comfortable as possible. Make up a travel package and send it to your visitors in advance.

Include in the package:
- A detailed map of your area showing the location of your office in relation to the airport.
- A list of good restaurants and motels (with phone numbers).

(*From Nine To Five*, Dartnell, 4660 Ravenswood Ave., Chicago, IL 60640-9981)

They'll remember you by the gifts you bear

Bring company products to seminars to advertise yourself. At recent BLC seminars:

- ☐ One editor from Hershey's brought candy bars for the afternoon break.
- ☐ A hospital PR person brought "I was born at _____ Hospital" t-shirts for all attenders.
- ☐ A member of the Egg Board brought key rings shaped like eggs for all attenders.
- ☐ An employee of a California distillery brought — yes! — selected bottles of wine for the hospitality suite.

Nothing wins immediate good will like a practical, useful gift that incorporates that giver's product or service. Remember, handing your business card to everyone you meet can get tiring after awhile.

The awesome power of words

Remember, when you take notes at a meeting you could be the most powerful person. Why? Because the process of most business negotiations needs to be written up in a memo or a report — if you control the note-taking and the writing of the memo then, in a way, you control the outcome of the meeting.

(*Business Horizons*)

Proper time for handouts

Don't place handouts on tables in advance of a meeting attended by people who don't know each other. Many will spend time reading the handouts instead of mingling and getting to know one another around the coffeee pot. On the other hand, don't distribute handouts during a talk or just before it. For obvious reasons. People will study the handouts instead of doing what they ought to be doing — listening to you.

Have participants introduce each other
When you ask people to introduce themselves at a meeting or seminar, ask them to speak to the person in the room seated farthest from them. This method guarantees that everyone else in the room will hear them. It also trains participants to project their voices.

Wear name tag on right
At meetings people usually wear name tags on the left side of their suit coats. It's best, however, to wear them on the right so the person you're greeting will look directly at your name when shaking hands.

(*Successful Meetings*, 633 Third Ave., New York, NY 10017)

Keep meetings short
Here's how to keep your meetings from turning into two- or three-hour ordeals:

■ If you want a meeting to last no longer than an hour, plan your agenda for 40 minutes. Give yourself a 20-minute cushion.

■ Reinforce your determination to keep it short by scheduling the meeting so that it ends close to a natural break in the day — lunch or the end of the working day.

(Adapted in part from *AUL News*, Corporate Communications, American United Life, One American Square, P.O. Box 368, Indianapolis, IN 46206-0368.)

Sit at table's head
In small group meetings the chairperson often refuses to sit at the head of a conference table, paying obeisance to a phony sense of egalitarianism. Don't make such a mistake when you're running the meeting. People can see you better. You present yourself as the leader. You can more easily determine the direction of the meeting.

Put people at ease
Want strangers attending a meeting to know each other quickly — and have a bit of icebreaking fun? Arrange people at tables made into a "U" so they're facing each other. Ask the first person sitting on your left to give his or her first name and say something personal. "I'm Alice, and I relax by standing on my head." The person sitting next to Alice says, "This is Alice who relaxes by standing on her head. I'm Jim. I run 10 miles every morning." Sitting next to Jim, Debbie says, "Alice stands on her head, Jim runs 10 miles every morning, and I'm Debbie. I have three grandchildren." And so on around the table. Although the exercise can be performed successfully with up to 40 or 50 people, 15 or 20 works best.

Be your own press agent

At a recent convention on Quality Circles, the representatives from Orange and Rockford Utilities came up with an idea anyone presenting a talk at a convention can use.

Because many groups were giving presentations at the same time, the Orange and Rockford Group wanted to make sure their talk was well attended.

They distributed printed invitations to all attenders the night before their talk.

Result: "An overflow crowd very receptive to their ideas and impressed by their skill," according to evaluations of the attenders.

Industry conventions often imply competition; you represent your company, whether you mean to or not.

(*Lamp Post*, One Blue Hill Plaza, Pearl River, NY 10965)

Get rid of the chairs to promote conversation

Are you trying to promote more interaction between people attending your conference? If you're planning a reception, take away the chairs. Replace them with elbow-high cocktail tables where attendees can stand and talk to each other without having to juggle drinks and plates of hors d'oeuvres.

(*The Meeting Manager*, 1950 Stemmons Freeway, Dallas, TX 75207-3109)

Call a meeting only if you must

Most successful meeting planners and leaders recommend that you avoid meetings whenever possible and deal with business in other ways. Some guidelines:

You don't need a meeting if:
- You always have one on a certain day but have nothing to discuss on that day.
- You're going to make a certain decision regardless of what anyone else says.

You need a meeting if:
- You have information to give to many people immediately, at the same time.
- You need a decision and don't have time to circulate memos.
- You need diverse points of view on an important issue.

(*How to Run a Meeting* by Bobbi Linkemer, American Management Association, 135 West 50th St., New York, NY 10020)

Prepare for your next trade show

After you have tested the equipment you're going to bring to the show, record the serial number of each component used in the dress rehearsal. When the equipment arrives, check the serial numbers again to make sure you have the right equipment.

(Leonard Hindus writing in *Successful Meetings*, 633 Third Ave., New York, NY 10017)

Organize a successful panel discussion

The biggest responsibility in a panel discussion falls to the chairperson. When this is your job, follow these six steps.

☐ Make sure you know three weeks in advance what topic each participant is going to discuss.

☐ Emphasize that when you say a panelist has ten minutes, you mean ten minutes, not twelve or fifteen or twenty.

☐ Have each panelist send in a prepared introduction of him or herself. This will save you time.

☐ Prepare questions for each panelist. Suggest to the participants that they come prepared with questions for other panelists.

☐ Prepare your summation. You need a strong conclusion to close the discussion.

☐ Two weeks before the event, send out a letter to your participants saying you hope they've prepared theirs talks (no one will have) on the topic discussed, conforming to the time frame you mentioned previosuly. Tell them you'll stick rigidly to the time allotment so they should be prepared to stay within it, and that a pre-arranged signal will mean the presentation should be concluding.

(Excerpted from *Never Be Nervous Again* by Dorothy Sarnoff, and cited in *Spirit*, East/West Network, Inc., 34 E. 51st St., New York, NY 10022)

Meeting planners: Avoid these mistakes

The most common marketing mistakes of meeting planners can be summed up in one sentence: "We underprice overly broad programs, mail out too few 'me too' brochures too late, and do not analyze results carefully." In greater detail:

1. **Underpricing:** "Your audience wants quality and is willing to pay for it."

2. **Overly broad programs:** "Focus your meetings more sharply. Don't try to be all things to all people."

3. **Too few brochures:** "Don't miss getting sufficient attendance because you haven't mailed far enough, high enough, or low enough."

4. **"Me Too" brochures:** "Be creative, be innovative, be bold."

5. **Too late:** "There is no magic formula for finding the optimum mailing date. But every day you go beyond that date is costing you registrations."

6. **Analyze results:** "Next time you'll do a better job of focusing your program, selecting your lists, and designing your brochure ... if you've tested and anlyzed the results carefully."

Looking for more marketing tips? These are from one of 79 "mini-reports" from the Marketing Federation, 109 58th Ave., St. Petersburg Beach, FL 33706, (813) 367-6545. The reports are $2 each, or $50 for all 79.

Bring your training workshops to life

A training workshop doesn't have to be boring. People learn best when they're actively participating, not learning by lecture or rote, so avoid putting your audience to sleep. Starting the session with small-group discussions can bring out comments and questions. Also, ask open-ended questions that don't put an emphasis on eliciting a "right" answer, and give "how-to" advice that's relevant to audience needs, using a case-study format to increase interest.

(Ron and Susan Zemke, "30 Things We Know for Sure about Adult Learning," cited in *American School Board Journal*, Alexandria, VA)

Draw crowds at trade shows — with popcorn

If you want to attract people to your booth or exhibit at a trade show, get a popcorn machine. The machine itself — find a big, brightly-colored one that lets people watch the corn pop — plus the popping sound, and the freshly-popped aroma, will draw interested potential customers from all over. Make sure you stuff the popcorn in bags that carry your logo and phone number.

Ask speaker for references

Find out what kind of group the speaker has addressed in the past, if he or she met the group's needs, and what the reaction to the message was.

(Secrets of a Successful Meeting, 1814 Commercenter West, Suite E., San Bernardino, CA 92408)

NEWS RELEASES

It's a basic part of the communicator's job, but putting out the organization's news in a form that will get it printed or aired is not as routine as some people think. Check out these tips on news releases that win editorial acceptance.

Guidelines for sending news releases

If you write news releases and want to increase your odds of getting them picked up by a major publication, here are a few guidelines to remember:

Know the editorial focus of your news story and of the publication you're sending the release. An obvious point, but still, the editors of BLC receive hundreds of news releases a week that have nothing to do with communication.

Use the phone as a follow up after sending news releases. Remember not to be unsure of yourself when talking to the editor. This might suggest that you're unsure of the product you're trying to publicize.

Make sure the outside of your package reflects the inside. If the outside is a fancy folder and the inside only a couple of photos of a groundbreaking ceremony, you're in trouble. Your job is to impress the editor.

Do's and don'ts for video

To make a video news release — or feature — it helps to build on subjects of most interest to a TV audience: money, health, and sex. Some guidelines:

- Stay in touch with TV editors who specialize in fashion, health, medical, etc.
- Call a variety of regional news directors and news assignment people in TV markets around the country to find out what formats they prefer.
- Don't include spokespeople from your own organization. Instead, get a sound bite from an authority in the field. Expecially useful and available are people from nonprofit organizations.
- Write the piece as a local TV writer would do the job — write the lead, the piece itself, the conclusion.
- Tie the piece to a news event, if possible—an anniversary, a milestone, a special week, etc.,
- Think about a multi-part series, because it takes relatively little extra money to make a five-part series rather than a single.

(Michael Klepper, Chaiman, Michael Klepper Associates, New York, at the annual conference of the International Assocaition of Business Communicators)

If you've got news, give it to them!

Package your news releases professionally so your recipients will consider them newsworthy, says John F. Budd, Jr., senior vice president of corporate communications, Emhart Corporation. Other suggestions from Budd:

Media kits should never include marketing or sales material — they are inappropriate for a news and information folder.

Photo captions should never spell out what people can plainly see for themselves; they should give readers a quick, clear explanation of the significance of the picture.

How to get on the 6 o'clock news

Advice on how to get TV assignment editors to notice your news releases.
1. **Follow up your news release with a call.** But never call within 30-60 minutes of the next newscast. To discuss coverage for the 6 pm news, call between 6 and 7:30 *in the morning*. That's generally when the newsroom is fairly quiet. If your event requires 11 pm news coverage, wait until after lunchtime to call — night editors don't start their shift until mid-afternoon.
2. **If your news item itself is marginal,** remember that visuals *can* sell the story. The difference between a 10-second copy story and a full-blown reporter package is frequently in the pictures.
3. **Assignment editors generally file** usable material by date — be sure the time, location and date are clearly indicated at the top tof the release.

(Kathryn Rainaldi, Crum and Forster Corp., Corporate Communications, 299 Madison Ave., Morristown, NJ 07960)

How to deal with the media
When writing news releases, refer to them as *news* releases, not press releases. *Why?* Because a press release is associated with PR people trying to publicize something and, consequently, the media don't see it as news.
(Adapted in part form *Pennsylvania Education*, 333 Market St., Harrisburg, PA 17126-0333)

Get your videos on the news
TV broadcasters still use free materials sent to them, especially to fill gaps in post-movie showings or when scheduled programs run short. The kinds of films they most prefer are sports and entertainment, followed by travel and recreation. Stories on health — third place. They prefer the format of 3/4-inch videocassettes. Preferred length is from 6 to 15 minutes.

Write for 10 PSA tips, FREE
The pamphlet, "How to Get More Cluck for the Buck," explains how to distribute television public service announcements (PSAs). It outlines "Ten Tips for More Effective PSA Campaigns." It includes information on videotape dub formats; station relations; distribution lists; and evaluation. Write for a free copy to Goodwill Communications, Suite 914, 1260 21st St., N.W., Washington, DC 20036.

Help reporters with NYSE symbol
If you write news releases, and your company is publicly held, remember to put your trading symbol on the New York Stock Exchange on the letterhead next to your company's name. The first thing many reporters will want to know is how your stock is doing. Knowing the NYSE symbol will help them find out.

Top editors want this kind of news
A survey of managing editors and publishers at over 10,000 U.S. newspapers by *News USA*, shows new trends:
☐ **Health information** of any kind is most popular, said 64 percent of the respondents.
☐ **Advice** from senior executives ran second at 58 percent.
☐ **Editorial cartoons** came in at 54 percent. This is 50% higher than requests for editorial comment.
☐ **Most desired length** is 250 words, said 55 percent.
☐ **Graphics, cartoons**, and photos are in high demand by 76 percent, 62 percent, and 58 percent respectively.
☐ **Almost all editors** want more consumer-oriented material.
   Editor's note: For a FREE copy of "Newspaper Survey Highlights" write: *News USA*, 1199 National Press Bldg., Washington, DC 20045.

Rules for writing better news releases

☐ **Put the best,** most important idea in your lead.
☐ **Be brief:** break up long sentences and keep paragraphs short.
☐ **Eliminate clutter:** look out for redundancy and extraneous facts.
☐ **Avoid generalities** and be as specific as possible. (*How* is your society working to improve dental health?)
☐ **Weed out adjectives** and adverbs; understatement goes a long way with the media. No one will believe your unique program is unique unless you show *how* the program is unusual.
☐ Again, the word is "understatement."

(*Communications Update,* American Dental Association, 211 East Chicago Ave., Chicago, IL 60611)

Know your audience: It's the key to success!

If you're promoting your company's new pay policy, you wouldn't send a news release to *The Johnny Carson Show*. You might, however, if you were promoting a client who just flew 100 yards in a bird suit. W*hy?* Because you know that *The Johnny Carson Show* deals with odd happenings, not serious issues.

The key to success, when promoting anything (clients, new publications, books, yourself, organizations, etc.) is to know your audience. It has been said before — but not enough.

Here, at the *Bottom Line Communicator*, we constantly get news releases that have nothing to do with our business. The news releases go from hand to garbage in one fluid motion, and yet, day after day, they keep coming. We wonder who's getting paid to waste so much time.

We emphasize: To be a sucessful marketer you don't need talent. It's hard work. It's knowing the markets that need what you're offering, and then taking the time to convince them that they *want* it. It's knowing your audience.

Be accessible

Include your home phone number in a news release that's especially timely or sent on short notice. It's a real convenience to reporters on a 10 p.m. deadline, and all journalists will appreciate your effort at accessibility — even if they don't need to take you up on it.

The importance of news releases

Never begin a news release with the fact of an announcement or the name of the person making the announcement if you want the release to be read.

For example: Don't say "Galactic Inc. President James Bux announced today that the company will expand its sales force by 5,000." Instead, begin with the newsworthy item: "Galactic Inc. will expand its sales force by 5,000, President James Bux announced today."

Photographs need words

Don't forget to write or rubberstamp your name, organization, and address on the back of any publicity photographs you send. An amazing number come to this office with no identification. When a picture is separated from the accompanying news release or story, editors will usually throw it away.

Another reminder: If you handwrite information on the reverse side of a glossy photo, be sure you do so in a way that your words do not mar the picture: use a thick felt pen, or write it in a corner.

Make releases easier to read

Fold your news release so that your nameplate, headline (if any), and lead sentence can be read as it comes out of the envelope. Don't fold the news release as you would a letter, with the contents folded inward. If you fold the release outward, you'll save the editor's time.

Go with your instincts

Don't be tyrannized by advice to write short news releases. Yes, of course, write them no longer than they should be. But they should not always be short, especially if you are summarizing a complex story or an important speech. Three double-spaced pages are not too much. The editor wants lots of good stuff from which to select. Also, in a metropolitan market with competing media, editors are less likely to pick out identical quotes.

Get the most from pictures

If you send out a news release promoting a new product, send two pictures of the product: One showing the product itself (emphasizing all its important features), the other showing someone *using* the product.

Ten steps to writing better news releases

1. Make it concise. Write crisply, in short words and sentences, using verbs in the active voice. Use the facts, but don't get mired in them.
2. Use a summary title.
3. State your purpose in the first paragraph.
4. Explain quickly and clearly why your news is important.
5. Include the time, date, and place.
6. Proofread carefully.
7. Mail it on time. If it's important enough, hand deliver it.
8. Send it to the right person.
9. Call the day before the event to be sure your news release has been received.
10. Don't waste the editor's time plugging a marginal story.

Write a better news story

Visualize your story as a miniskirt: short enough to be interesting but long enough to cover all the vital points. Don't be so brief, that you leave any who, what, where, why, or how questions unanswered.

Use nicknames only when they are necessary to identify someone, and never when they're obvious (e.g. Robert "Bob" Brown).

Don't let titles cloud your narrative; if you need to identify someone as Vice President and Director of Marketing and Public Relations, take a separate sentence to do so.

Use "said" almost always. State, claimed, asserted, charged, averred — they all draw attention to themselves and away from the speaker's words.

Never be afraid to ask a source to define a term. Not understanding something is no disgrace; not trying to understand something is.

(*101 Memos for Reporters* by Ed Arnold, 212 W. Superior Street, Chicago, IL 60610)

Five steps to getting your letter published

Want to write a letter to the editor of your local newspaper and see it published? Here are some simple rules developed by Ted Carroll, an editorial page editor of the *Florida Times-Union*, who outlined them in an article in the *Conservative Digest*.
- Follow the guidelines specified by the paper.
- Type the letter.
- Make it attractive — double-space, use wide margins.
- Work, work, work, on your letter — be grammatical and concise.
- Never on Sunday! It will get lost in the Monday morning deluge of mail.

Useful phrase for news release writers

'Has announced' is a phrase with many advantages for those who write news releases. For example:

"William Witenkowski, president of XYZ Products, has announced the appointment of Stanley Jones as vice president of public relations."

The phrase is apt because it implies the news value of immediacy, but does not require a specific date.

In the present perfect tense, the phrase tells of an action carried out in the past and completed in the present.

Send it overnight for immediate attention

Want to get your story/letter/press release noticed? Send it in an overnight delivery package. Express Mail, Federal Express, Purolator, and their competitors all command immediate attention when they're received. They're opened and read quickly, and if your material is good, you'll get a faster response than you would by sending it regular mail.

Getting the media's attention

Are your mailings being discarded before being regarded? They may well be: editors and producers are deluged with releases daily. To help your information stand apart from the rest:

- Develop thematic communiques, e.g., a target-shaped pamphlet on target marketing.
- Think big: giant-size packages won't be ignored. Incorporate small messages into one big one. Got a lot of news? — Put it into a single attractive package that will need to gain attention only once.
- Deliver it in person, but only if it's really special news.

(*pr reporter*, Dudley House, P.O. Box 600, Exeter, NH 03833)

NONPROFITS

Their special needs, especially in the field of appeals for funds, are addressed in this section. Some of the tips may surprise you.

Direct-mail fundraising tips

- Encourage credit-card giving — donation values will jump about 25%.
- Keep a list of your "Top 100" donors on your desk, and make it a habit to phone two a day just to say thanks — with no pitch.
- Send donors tax receipts — and use the opportunity to make another appeal.

Cutting costs and making money

☐ If your agency is on a limited budget, create an annual report that doubles as a general information handout. Include your mission statement, philosophy, and other general information so that when people read the report, they'll have a good idea of what your agency is trying to accomplish.

☐ Before developing a publication, identify the exact purpose of why you're doing so. Are you trying to raise money or is your publication's use going to be strictly informational? Once you decide, you'll know what to include and what not to include.

☐ When planning fundraising events for the future, make your events annual. That way, people will come to expect your fundraiser at a certain time of the year and plan for it.

☐ When planning your annual report, use charts and diagrams to show financial information. Include income comparisons over the years and projections for the future. People will trust your agency if they feel you are on solid ground financially and are organized enough to prove that fact on paper.

(Allen Selinski, Guadalupe Area Project, St. Paul, MN 55107)

More great ways to raise money

Raising money is a tough task for any nonprofit organization. Asking people to give money without offering them something of material value in return can cause many headaches. Allen Selinski, director of development at Guadalupe Area Project in St. Paul, Minn., offers some ideas.

☐ **When writing thank you letters to donors,** include some inside information about your agency. Doing this keeps donors informed, and makes them feel they're an important part of your organization.

☐ **Include the amount of donation in your thank you letter.** Donors will be able to use it as a receipt for tax purposes.

☐ **Personally sign as much correspondence as is humanly possible.** Selinski asks, "When was the last time you checked to see if a letter you received was signed, and were pleased that it was?" He advises: "Use the media to your advantage. If you have a large mailing going out, attempt to sign every letter personally and inform the media beforehand that you're going to do it."

☐ **When you spend money on an expensive brochure,** be sure to leave out specific events and dates. "There's nothing worse than reading through a brochure you intended to use for a long period of time and then realizing it is outdated soon after it was printed."

Survey shows why readers get annoyed

BLC editors have examined more than 600 non-periodicals. In more than 200, there was no address or phone number.

Incredibly, most of these pieces were part of a fundraising campaign. Had any of these pieces been persuasive enough to motivate the reader to give money, a significant number of potential donors wouldn't know where to send their gifts.

It may well be that in the original mailing other pieces gave the address. Or the original envelope may have been saved. But never assume that every piece of mailing will be kept or kept together.

The rule: Each piece in a fundraising effort must be self-contained.

In a survey conducted by the School of Mass Communications at Virginia Commonwealth University, the absence of address or phone number was listed as the major annoyance of readers.

Gift offers may backfire on donation appeals

Why do people help other people? Appalachian State University marketing professors Bonnie Guy and Wesley Patton point out that we have a basic instinct to help people without expectation of any reward. So, tax breaks or special gift offers may actually cause potential donors to resist the urge to support your nonprofit organization. Instead, emphasize the nonmaterial benefits of giving.

(*Purview*, a supplement of *pr reporter*, P.O. Box 600, Exeter, NH 03833)

PERSONAL RELATIONS

Getting along with fellow workers (that includes the boss) is basic to success. You may not want to be elected Miss or Mr. Personality Kid, but just getting your work done can involve knowing how to deal with others.

Great employee relations: 'I am my company!'

Among the most effective advertisements in the country are the ones that show one member of the National Rifle Association with the headline: "I am the NRA." As the summer picnic season nears, here's a way you can adapt that technique for a great employee gift: a t-shirt with the corporate logo on one side and on the other: "I am (name of company)." For instance: "I am Mobil Oil."

Getting the constituent — employee, shareholder, customer, community resident — to see the company as people like himself or herself has always been one valid goal of good communication.

Retired workers are important

Don't forget your retired employees. Follow the call of Southern Bell in Florida: It revitalized a ho-hum publication, *Retirees Newsletter*, and, in conducting a readership survey, found that 77% of the respondents said they always read it; 90% rated the content good or excellent; and 47% said they wanted it expanded.

Never forget the losers

If you have contests, remember the losers or next time you might not have any winners. When Children's Holiday had an art contest it sent a set of markers and a package of drawing paper to every loser with the following letter.

"I have good news and bad news. The bad news is that you didn't win the Children's Holiday Art Contest. The good news is that we enjoyed your work so much that we want you to have the enclosed markers and drawing paper. Please try again next year."

(Wendy Berninger, Matthew Bender & Co., Inc., 1274 Broadway, Albany, NY 12201)

Give more, and get more from your secretaries

Secretaries' knowledge of their company's goals and objectives is too often limited to what they can glean from the papers that cross their desks. Make your secretary a part of the team, urges Betsy Lazary, author of *How to Find, Hire and Keep a Good Secretary*. Take these steps:
• Invite your secretary to meetings — not just to take notes, but for informational purposes.
• Frequently update your secretary on the status of ongoing projects, regardless of whether immediate action is required by either of you.
• Set aside time with your secretary just to talk about work — upcoming projects, new directions, potential problem areas.

PR executives do best as moral managers

It's heartening to see a call for the best talent in public relations as one method to attain moral objectives within the organization.

Writes Clarence C. Walton in *The Moral Manager*: "Since executives seek to 'manage' their contacts with ideologies in ways designed to preserve and promote their organizations' well-being, their public relations departments need the best, not second-best, talent. Such talent should have regular consistent access to the CEO even as it is regularly and consistently accessed by the 'boss'"

If it is PR people who must organize messages sent through the organization, Walton recommends that they:

- <u>Send a president's message</u> regularly through in-house media to explain the organization's expectations for employees' on-the-job as well as off-the-job behavior in public places.
- <u>Feature stories</u> on employees who have reacted with moral conviction when faced by an ethical problem arising within the organization.
- <u>Provide incentives</u> and rewards for employees who have helped the organization to become more efficient and more ethical.
- <u>Review the organization's code</u> of ethics, using managers and workers to do so. Then share their assessments with other employees.
- <u>Schedule lunches</u> in which managers may meet specialists to discuss ideas concerning organizational moral development.

(*The Moral Manager* by Clarence C. Walton, Balinger Publishing Co., Cambridge, MA 02138; $24.95)

Six decisions to make before you hire

A well-written job description helps you in both hiring people and promoting them. Here are some guidelines:

1. **Decide what's required.** Think in terms of results, not just performance.
2. **Focus on basics.** What are the employee's duties? Who will the employee be accountable to?
3. **Describe the minimum qualifications for the job.** This will help you target desirable applicants and screen out others.
4. **Summarize the position** in one paragraph. Be simple and straightforward.
5. **List the specific duties** and responsibilities of the job, beginning with the most important on down. Write concisely, but be thorough.
6. **Explain the organization's structure** and its chain of authority. This will eliminate confusion later on.

Be sure to avoid ambiguous words or phrasings. Like a resume, one page is the proper length of a job description. Also like a resume, the job description should be reviewed and updated regularly.

(*Human Resources Update*, Dartnell, 4660 Ravenswood, Chicago, IL 60640)

Know who speaks a second language

Create a document that lists the educational background of employees: their professional memberships and accreditations; volunteer involvement; second language, and other such data that could be helpful to the company some day.

Hire an intern

Hiring an intern can save you money, and propel a young student's career. Here are some questions to be considered:
1. Can you or a staff member devote time to the student?
2. Will your staff accept the idea?
3. Can you give the student meaningful work — something that he or she learns from, and at the same time saves you money?

(Society of Natl. Assn. Publications, 1010 Wisconsin Ave., Washington, DC 20007)

Don't play the negative communicator's game

The "negative communicator" manipulates those who play the game. Know the tactics and you'll gain the upper hand.

The constant interrupter: They gradually dominate the conversation by simply wearing you down. **Counterattack:** Get back to specifics. Your reply should address *exactly* how you think the client will react to *each detail* of the approach.

The Martyr: This person establishes him or herself as the hardest-working, longest-suffering employee in the company. The implication, of course, is that everyone else is a laggard. **Counterattack:** Agree with his or her claims of hard work, and add a positive comment about how widespread that attitude seems to be among others in the department.

The advice-giver: This person is full of great ideas, most of which would fall flat in practice. If you don't act on each one, you're "tentative," or worse. **Counterattack:** Thank your friend for the advice, go back to the source with a casual reminder — in detail, including the date — of his or her "fine" idea.

(*Supervisory Management*, 22 Bore St., Lichfield, Staffs, Ws13-6LP, England)

Pad waiting period for happy clients, bosses

When you have to make customers or colleagues wait, take a cue from the managers at Walt Disney Attractions. Walt Disney World posts exaggerated waiting times for each attraction so that guests eager to go through "It's A Small World" are pleasantly surprised at having to wait only fifteen minutes, not the twenty-five that's posted. Similarly, if you tell your boss you'll have that report ready on Friday when you know you can finish by Wednesday, the boss will be impressed and grateful when you deliver it two days ahead of time.

(*Newsweek*)

Learn to say 'No' to save time and stress

The temptation to agree to work on every new project can be pretty powerful, but if you commit yourself to too many tasks, you'll drain yourself of the time and energy you need to do your own job effectively. Learn to say "No" with help from the following:

■ Say no quickly—before people start to think you're going to say yes. Avoid "I don't know," or "Let me think about it." Delaying your answer only increases the chances of an angry reaction later.

■ Say no pleasantly and politely: Don't alienate the person you're turning down by being curt, rude, or defensive.

■ Say no, but offer an alternative. "I won't chair that meeting for you, Bill, but I'll be happy to attend and present some ideas."

■ Remember, you have the right to say no. If you're not being ordered by a superior, then you're under no obligation to spend extra time and energy on a task that's above and beyond your own responsibilities on the job—and you have no obligation to justify your refusal.

(*The Effective Executive,* Dartnell, 4660 Ravenswood, Chicago, IL 60640)

Refuse interruptions politely and effectively

Let people know that you don't want to be interrupted without offending them. For example, when someone asks "Do you have a minute?" calmly say, "No, I really don't. Can I get back to you in x minutes?" Then make sure you call back when you say you're going to. Reinforce your message by respecting other people's time and not interrupting them unless absolutely necessary.

(*Successful Self-Management,* Crisp Publications, Inc., 95 First Street, Los Altos, CA 94022)

Get yourself noticed using 'personal relations'

PR isn't just "public" relations. It can also be "personal" relations — a communications program aimed at improving your personal stature within your company and your field. Consultant Alfred Geduldig, former president of the communications firm Chester Burger Co., suggests you take these actions today, and watch your stock rise tomorrow:

- Call your company's communications department, or a trade journal in your field, and offer to write an article.
- Tell the same people about awards or other recognition you've earned for yourself or for your company.
- Seek out a project with high company visibility — no matter how unpleasant it may be. Complete it successfully, and the exposure will be worth it.
- Join an employee committee in your company.
- Encourage invitations to speak before community or trade groups, and, if appropriate, provide a courtesy copy of your remarks to top management.

Reduce stress in 30 seconds

You don't always have time to go swimming — or take a vacation — when you're feeling overstressed, so here's a quick, simple relaxation exercise that should help:

Sit back with both feet on the floor, your hands in your lap. Close your eyes. Breathe in, focusing on cool air; exhale, focusing on warm air. Raise your shoulders and tighten them; tighten your fists, too. Breathe deeply and hold it for five seconds. Exhale slowly while lowering your shoulders and relaxing your fists. Roll your shoulders backward three or four times. Now, get back to work.

(*Progress,* Baylor University Medical Center, 3500 Gaston Ave., Dallas, TX 75246)

An information gathering place

If you want people to read internal news on the bulletin board, place the coffee machine beside it. You'll find that this is one of the best places in your organization for people to gather and learn about what's going on in their company.

Communicate with your peers

"Most managers give a lot of thought to the way they approach their bosses — and their staff," says Ellen Belzer in *Working Woman* magazine. "They know the importance of mastering upward and downward communications skills. Unfortunately, many managers neglect lateral communications with their colleagues in other departments." Belzer lists these suggestions for honing a manager's skills at networking "sideways."

☐ **Venture beyond your circle of pals.** Visit one or two of your peers in other departments each week and think about what information you might obtain each visit.

☐ **Plan a managers' forum.** Once or twice a year, this allows time for discussion about common areas of interest.

☐ **Do favors.** Offer the services of your department to other managers when they're in a crunch. Later, when you need some help, the other department managers will be happy to pitch in.

☐ **Identify communication glitches.** Are you receiving information from other departments on a timely basis, or after the fact? Discuss these issues with your peers in other departments.

☐ **Involve senior management.** Although you normally don't need approval to meet informally with other managers, let senior management know about your plans for improving horizontal communications so your actions aren't misinterpreted—and so you get the proper credit when it's due.

Different ways to communicate with employees

Employee communication is more than the company publication. Here are some additional ways to supplement your program:

☐ <u>Video magazines.</u> Video is becoming less expensive. And even if your company doesn't have professional A/V people, you will find many in the organization whose hobby is shooting and producing video films. Motivate them to produce a quarterly video magazine about their fellow employees—achievements at work, hobbies, sports, etc.

☐ <u>Face-to-face sessions.</u> Develop manager-employee feedback sessions. Choose and announce the subject of each session in advance, and ask employees to bring ideas, problems, or solutions to the meetings. Warning: don't allow the session to be manipulated by the highest-ranking participants—or the purpose will be lost.

☐ <u>Posters.</u> You can buy them or design them to fit your particular occasion.

☐ <u>Banners.</u> Surprise employees one morning with a banner outside the office. An example might be: "Save a Life Today, Give Blood."

☐ <u>Promotional items.</u> You can order all kinds of items printed with a message on them: calendars, paperweights, shirts, pens, etc.

(*Work Dynamics*)

Ask a third party to join your conversations

Create a more relaxed atmosphere for a potentially stressful confrontation by inviting a third person to sit in on delicate conversations. This will change the dynamics of the situation by placing your behavior, and that of the other person, under the scrutiny of a third party. Also, this will increase self-awareness and sensitivity, giving both of you the feeling of being protected by the presence of the "witness."

(*The Pleasure of Your Company: A Socio-Psychological Analysis of Modern Society*, by Ernie Pin, Praeger, 521 Fifth Avenue, New York, NY 11175)

Five tips for remembering names

Do you have trouble remembering names of people you've just met? Many of us do. Here are some tips:

1. **Listen** and make sure you hear the name accurately.
2. **Spell** the name out loud.
3. **Think** of a visual device that will help you recall the new name. If Mr. Appleton is a portly man, imagine him eating *apples* by the *ton*.
4. **Comment** on the name ("I know someone else who spells her name exactly that way."
5. **Use** the name one more time when you say good-bye.

(*Communications for Results*, by Cheryl Hamilton and Cordell Parker, Belmont, CA 1987, cited in *The Pryor Report*, P.O. Box 1766, Clemson, NC 29633)

Persuasion at its best

When you're trying to persuade people, never directly contradict them; it will make your task harder. Ben Franklin, a master statesman, forbade himself words like certainly and undoubtedly. "I adopted instead I conceive, I apprehend, or I imagine a thing to be so and so; or so it appears to me at present," Franklin said. If you abruptly disagree with someone, you'll embarrass them or put them on the defensive.

(*Speak Out with Clout*, Magna Publications, Inc., Box 286, Cabin John, MD 20818)

Exercise 20 minutes a day

A recent study shows that employees with poor lifestyle habits have the highest medical bills. Health care costs for obese people were 11% higher than those for people of normal weight.

- Encourage employees to exercise at least 3 times a week, 20 minutes per day.
- Start a "Health Newsletter."
- Offer rewards for people who go on a diet and lose weight.
- Have a 10 minute workout twice a day.

Get people involved in exercise and some could realize how out-of-shape they are — some might even become health fanatics.

(Adapted in part from the *Wall Street Journal* cited in *Pace*, One Baxter Parkway, Deerfield, IL 60015)

Boosting morale need not be expensive

Try these ways to communicate with employees and to provide a working environment that will make people happy.

Write happy-birthday notes to employees ... Hold regular informal meetings between employees and managers to advance understanding ... Create a community project in which employees and managers can work together ... Use the supervisor to introduce new employees to their co-workers.

More: Hang a plaque in the lobby announcing anniversary dates of employees ... Keep in touch with retirees by way of an annual breakfast ... Invite part-time employees to all social events ... Send commendation letters when employees perform outstandingly, and place copies of such letters in their personnel folders.

More: Organize flexible working hours during slow periods ... Hold orientation meetings for new employees ... Develop a program honoring the "Employee of the Week" or "Employee of the Month."

And a few more: Decorate eating areas for special occasions ... Dispense free coffee on special days ... Hold a reception or small party for every retiring employee ... Give awards for employees who are commended by customers.

(*The Effective Executive*, Dartnell Corp., 4660 Ravenswood Ave., Chicago, IL 60640)

Hiring interns is a good idea

An internship program enhances the image of your organization as community-minded. And it makes the intern a credible and enthusiastic spokesperson for your organization.

About half of all interns will become employees at the place where they interned. That pre-testing enables the communicator to hire staffers after seeing their capabilities. It eliminates the need for a probationary period. And if the intern doesn't work out, the trauma of being fired from a regular job is avoided.

A few tips:

☐ Don't use the intern as a go-fer. Allow him or her to apply classroom knowledge on the job.

☐ The student must have one supervisor who will review his or her work closely.

☐ Resist the temptation to say, "Here. Let me do it for you. I can do it more quickly than I can explain it."

☐ Make the work as varied as possible.

☐ To find interns, contact the Public Relations department at a local high school or college.

Eight ways people can tell you're not listening

1. You don't look them in the eye.
2. Your posture is dreadful—slumped in your chair, etc.
3. Your excessive notetaking borders on preoccupation.
4. You've placed objects in the line of sight between you, such as a notepad, tape recorder, purse, sheaf of papers.
5. You dress to call attention to yourself: sloppily, seductively, or outrageously.
6. You keep interrupting.
7. Your questions are long, overdefined, and rambling.
8. You never repeat your understanding of anything said or use respondent's words in phrasing your succeeding questions.

Are you a leader?

Here are three ways to tell if your leadership style is effective. When you are talking to people watch to see if:
- **Their eye contact with you is good.**
- **They face you in a relaxed state.**
- **Their voice is relaxed and calm.**

"Oversupervised" people look at the ceiling, turn their bodies away from their supervisors, and speak in a loud, sometimes sarcastic voice.

(Ken Blanchard writing in *Today's Supervisor*, 1108 O St., Sacramento, CA 95814)

Would they like to talk to the top guns?

Some of your people would probably like to talk with the executives they usually see only from a distance. But they don't know how to go about it.

Make it easy for them to do so by forming a Face-to-Face Communication Program. Merely print a simple coupon in your organizational publication. Or tack a sheaf of coupons to your bulletin boards. Leave room for the employee's name, job, title, and job location. The words are simple: "I would like to participate in a face-to-face session with...." Include titles of officers, managers, directors, etc., not excluding the top person at your location.

See how New England Electric does the job. Write Ann Johnson, 25 Research Dr., Westborough, MA 01582.

Be mean, lean, and CLEAN!

For the cleanest office in the building find out the name of the person who cleans your office.

- Every Friday, leave him or her a friendly note.
- Once a quarter, write a personalized thank-you note.
- When it's least expected—not at the holidays—leave a small present.

Check for hidden jargon

To improve communication, check your speech and writing for hidden jargon. Hidden jargon looks like plain speech, but isn't. It can cripple something as down-to-earth as selling insurance. Insurance salespeople routinely baffle prospects by using such common terms as "the insured," "face amount," "estate," and "rider." Get a friend outside your line of business to listen to your speech or presentation for hidden jargon. Especially watch for innocent-looking plain words that have a technical meaning.

(Adapted in part from an article by Andrew Byrne in *The State Life Bulletin*, State Life Ins. Co., 141 E. Washington St., Indianapolis, IN 46204.)

Give people choices

Did you know that as long as people *feel* they have a choice they'll produce more? A recent experiment proves this: A group of adults were asked to put together some difficult puzzles and proofread dull copy *while they listened to tapes of raucous noise*; half the participants had a choice of pushing a button to stop the noise.

The results were shocking: the group who had a choice of stopping the noise solved five times more puzzles and their proofreading had only one-fourth the errors of the other group—*and not once did the people with the buttons use them.*

(*Management World*)

Encourage employees to write letters to you

Gerry Mitchell, chairman of Dana Corp. — a $3.7 billion auto parts manufacturer — places posters everywhere, the caption reading, "Write a letter to your chairman." On the bottom left-hand corner of the poster is a thick pad of tear sheets, already stamped and addressed to Mitchell. He receives 3,000 letters a year. He reads and answers every one.

"In general," says Mitchell, "American management is no goddamn good at talking to people and listening."

(Business Week)

One use for passive voice

Use the passive voice to avoid assigning blame and embarrassing an employee who has made a mistake.
Use: "The box of parts was dropped inadvertently."
Not: "Smith dropped the parts."

Public speakers: consider this question

Here's a question always to be considered when communicating: *Does my audience share my assumptions?* The easiest way to upset people exists when your assumptions are so deep-seated that you never question whether others share them. **An example:** At a late morning church service on a Sunday in February the minister says, "I won't talk long, because I know all of you want to go home for the Super Bowl?" Do we? Does everybody in the church want to see the game? Are there some people bored by the idea?—you bet there are, a lot of them, and the speaker's inability to recognize that fact shows how difficult good communication really is.

PHOTOGRAPHS — TAKING

If taking photographs, or directing photographers, is part of your job, these handy tips may save time and money and improve the appearance of your printed material.

How to take better pictures

Remember this "rule of thumb" when taking group pictures: *don't leave enough room for your thumb between the heads of the people pictured.* Take the shot from the side, not from the front. That will force the people farthest from you to "peer around" those closest to you, eliminating the space between heads.

(Phil Douglis, *The Douglis Visual Workshops*, 212 S. Chester Rd., Swarthmore, PA 19081)

What to do about grip-and-grins

BLC readers who edit publications occasionally ask us what to do with grip-and-grin pictures — those ceremonial, ritualistic hand-shaking pictures that usually are a bore. Here are a few ideas.
1. **Don't use the picture.** Give the picture to the people affected. Give them a few extras, if necessary. But it's probably impractical to think that the problem will be solved that easily.
2. **Demand that the people stand close to each other.** Make them shake hands at a level with their chests. Then crop the picture into one column, thus minimizing the damage. *Don't* permit them to stand five feet from each other, their hands barely touching. That may mean a three-column picture!
3. **Use an appropriate symbol as a prop.** Enlarge the check to gigantic proportions. Have three people grasping the trophy. Put the plaque on the wall and have people look at it. You're right, those pictures won't win prizes or hang on museum walls, but they're better than the standard grip-and-grin.
4. **Encourage people in the picture to talk with each other.** Then take their picture. They're tongue-tied? Tell them to repeat after you, "Now is the time for all good men to come to the aid of their party," the old typewriting exercise. They'll begin to laugh and yuk it up. Take their picture while they're doing so. Don't permit them to look at you.
5. **Take many pictures.** Take them from many angles, up high, down low, up close (but not far away). Don't be afraid to shoot a small roll of film with the hope that you'll get a natural, effective picture.

Tilt your camera for better photos

Want to get 50 percent more out of your photographs? Tilt the camera so that one corner of the viewfinder points straight down. Instead of a horizontal picture, with a house or a boat in the middle and lots of unnecessary room above and beneath, you've got a diamond-shaped shot that gets every detail without any wasted space.

(*The Palm Branch*, 8001 Baymeadows Way, Jacksonville, FL)

Taking pictures of people who wear glasses

☐ Ask the person to dangle the glasses in his or her hand. If the subject is a man, you can get variety by asking him to hike one leg up on a chair, lean on his elbow, with his hand holding the glasses loosely.

☐ If it seems natural, ask the subject to push the glasses up on the forehead.

☐ Hand a cleansing tissue to the person and ask that he or she clean the glasses. Then take the picture as they are doing so.

☐ Finally, keep the glasses right where they should be. But don't forget to avoid the possibility of light bouncing off them and creating a glare.

Increase your visibility

If you take pictures at conferences for your press releases or corporate publications, avoid the humdrum shot of a person standing behind a lectern.

- Show one or two people in the audience reacting to the speaker. The effect of the speaker on the audience implies two-way communication.
- If you are using a hotel lectern, cover the name on the lectern with either your corporate logo or the title of the speech. Don't give free publicity.

PHOTOGRAPHS — USING

Now you have the photographs, what are you going to do with them? Especially the ones you'd really prefer not to use at all!

Be of good cheer; there are ways to minimize, if not eliminate, the problems photographs can create for an editor.

How to avoid photo cliches

☐ **Problem:** Too many photographs of people getting awards. All the photos look the same.
☐ **Diagnosis:** Photographs aren't meant to recognize achievement; they're meant to inspire imitation.
☐ **Political realities:** People in achievement photos want those photos.
☐ **Solution:** Give the awards photos to people in them. For your publication, use one or two of the award winners, photographed doing the thing for which they are being recognized — but not in the act of recognition.

Theme calendar promotes quality

The next time you have an "employee photo contest," ask employees to submit pictures on what quality means to them. *Why?* By having a theme calendar you'll promote company goals rather than a hodgepodge of photos that say nothing.

(*The 55 Biggest Communications Problems That Affect Your Bottom Line — And How You Can Solve Them,* by the editors of *BLC*)

Don't crop the joints!

Two tips to follow when cropping photos:

- Never crop a photographic subject at any body joint, especially the wrist or the ankle.
- If you're cropping at the top, crop between the hairline and the eyebrows. Don't just skim off part of the subject's head. And for a tight profile, crop in front of the ear. If the subjects are full length, crop at the bottom of the rib cage.

How to make photos effective

A crummy picture will always be a crummy picture, no matter how you doctor it — so don't think of improving the image. Find what is worth publishing in the picture, and then focus the reader's attention on the point you're trying to make. Six tricks:
1. **Tilt the picture** at an angle on the page.
2. **Make it appear** to "float" above the surface of the paper by casting a shadow.
3. **Frame the image** with hairline rules.
4. **Mutilate** the paper of which the photo is made. Turn a corner over, curl it in some way, tear off an edge.
5. **Combine several** pictures by an informal arrangement of overlaps to make them appear as though they had fallen onto the page.
6. **Reduce size** of pictures run them at the foot of the page, and don't attempt to catch attention with them. Use instead a big headline or some other technique.

(*Mastering Graphics, Design and Production Made Easy*, by Jan V. White; R.R. Bowker Co., New York and London)

Develop a photo file

If you use photographs in your publication, make it a point to develop a photo file of all the photographs you receive from public relations firms and agencies that mail to you. Also, try to obtain photographs from local chambers of commerce and other non-profit organizations in your area.

If some of the photos don't look the best, not to worry: there are many design tricks — severe cropping, for example — you can create with photos that will enhance their image. If you collect as many photos as you can, you'll be able to recognize when something will work in your publication.

(Cary Campbell, writing in *Magazine Issues*, ZedCoast Center, 1680 SW Bayshore Blvd., Port St. Lucie, FL 34984)

Use two photos for publication

The best photograph for a news story may be two pictures. Instead of always locking yourself into picking just one photo, look for combinations that achieve certain effects:
☐ Contrast. Use photos to highlight similarities in apparently dissimilar subjects, and differences between similar subjects.
☐ Close-up and context. A close-up of a specific person or object can complement an overall shot of the general scene.
☐ Sequence. Two or more pictures show action unfolding. Be sure they're all from the same vantage point, though.

(Daryl R. Moen, *Newspaper Layout and Design,* 2nd Edition, Iowa State University Press, Ames, IA 50010)

Avoid photos that are static, dull, and BORING

Experts advise editors to print photos that show action, that were taken with imagination, that are significant to the story.

That's what the experts say. But, realistically, how many editors are blessed with an abundance of interesting and exciting photos? How many editors have a photographer on the staff who can take them? Not many. Most editors fall prey to the same syndrome — take what you can get!

Usually what they get are static, dull, undesirable photos: grip-and-grinners, mug shots, group settings, poses, award presentations, desk shots, and pictures of the boss to name a few. Even worse — some editors try to print them all! If you're lucky, you may get a few interesting action shots, the rest mediocre. What can you do about this?

The simplest and most beneficial solution is to reduce the number of photos in your publication by eliminating some of the undesirables. This will allow you to increase the size of the remaining, more interesting photos and make not only your pages, but also your entire publication more attractive and interesting.

(Ed Arnold, design consultant, author, professor, 3208 Hawthorne, Richmond, VA 23222)

PRINTING MECHANICS

The job isn't done when the copy has been typed and the headlines written. Now comes the *really* hard part — putting it in a form that wins readership. From layout through proofreading and on to printing, the editor faces a multitude of decisions. These hints can help.

The right kind of paper can affect your message

The effect of paper on the message is so great than anyone communicating in print should know these findings by the American Paper Institute.

☐ Miami (Ohio) University did a fund-raising mailing to parents of current students. When a textured white stock and a regular white offset stock carrying the same message were mailed, the textured paper brought in more donors (13.1 percent) and money (16.8 percent) than the plain paper. Each additional dollar spent for the textured paper brought in an extra $8.74.

☐ The 3M Company sent a 6 3/4-by-10 1/2-inch letter and a business reply card. Half of the recipients — 5,000 of them — received a reply card printed on white index stock. The other half received the same card printed on grey vellum cover stock. All other elements remained the same. They grey textured cards brought 19.2 percent more responses. For every additional dollar spent for the colored and textured paper, there was additional business volume of $825.

(*Intermarket*, P.O. Box 285, Dayton, OH 45401)

When advertising, know the right color

Colors differ in the response they arouse in people, so when selecting colors for advertising, select the one that fits the promotion's goals.
 The major impacts of colors are as follows:
- **Red:** action color.
- **Yellow:** denotes happiness and sunshine; provides a glowing kind of frame for products.
- **Primary blue and green:** blues of sky and water evoke tranquility.
- **Earth tones:** imply trust because they are found in nature.

(*The 55 Biggest Communications Problems That Affect Your Bottom Line*, by the Editors of *TWC*)

Ten ideas to improve your layout

1. In a picture story, one picture should dominate your spread. It should be at least twice the size of the next largest picture. It should be your best picture.
2. Your page layout should be like a clothesline — straight across the top, but not necessarily aligned at the bottom. A scalloped layout ("ragged bottom") is OK if used consistently. It's informal, relaxed, contemporary. And easy.
3. Make all heads flush left in your newspaper or newsletter design. They are easy to write. They are contemporary; they give your page consistency.
4. Set the beginning of every story flush left. The first word in the lead paragraph aligns exactly, up and down, with the flush left head above it. That way, nothing interferes with the reader's movement into the story.
5. Headlines should always be above the story — never below it or to its side. Headlines should never be above pictures. *Why?* The reader's eye goes first to the boldness of other words, the editor is forcing erratic eye movements. Don't let it happen.
6. In magazine layouts (where such mistakes usually appear) never place a headline at the bottom of the page. Beginning at the bottom of the page, the reader's eye fights gravity, then is forced upward to the beginning of the story. If the story is good, the reader may go through that trouble. But it's possible the eyes will read the head and then go right off the page, prompting the reader to turn to the next page without having more than glanced at the display with the headline at the bottom.
7. Always remember, we read from left to right and from top to bottom. Keep that incontrovertible fact in mind when designing your pages.
8. Remember the printer's axiom: Bold is good, but all bold is no bold.
9. In a newsletter, one box is good, but two boxes on the same page are too much of a good thing.
10. If you have a choice, use Roman type for your body copy. Nothing beats it for readability.

Use boxes to highlight important items

The quickest, easiest, most effective way to draw attention to a small, important item: put a box around it. You can highlight by using boxes in a designed business letter or an informal newsletter. But when you use boxes, remember:

- **All emphasis is no emphasis.** Don't box everything. Use no more than one box per two pages.
- **Never fill in a box with a percentage of ink.** Screens and tint blocks make reading difficult.

(Tammy Oakes, Design Consultant, 550 Arlington, Chicago, IL 60605)

Consider quality of paper

When choosing the paper to use for your publication, consider these six points:

1. **Contrast between the ink and the paper.** The type should be sharp and clear so the reader can see it easily.
2. **Know what type of printing process is used.** It's impossible to print offset on letterpress stock.
3. **Paper should be sufficiently opaque.** This is important if you use many photographs, dark inks, and bold headlines.
4. **What can you afford?** Paper costs can range from 18% to 30% of a publication budget. And what about mailing? The heavier the paper, the more costly the mailing.
5. **Make sure the paper is durable.** Ask yourself: Does the color, texture, and brightness strike the proper mood and leave the impression you're hoping for? Is it heavy enough to wear repeated handling by readers, and durable enough to last for years?
6. **Will the print be easy to read?** Dull-finish papers, for example, are easier to see than high gloss papers.

(Robert L. Baker, editor of *Impact*, P.O. Box 1896, Chicago, IL 60204)

Red, blue, and black on yellow

When deciding on a color for the brochure, sales letter, or magazine spread, remember that people respond to color according to their age.

■ Children like red, yellow, and orange. Yellow gives way to green when they become college students.

■ What colors do almost everybody like? Red and blue. The elderly will tend to like blue more.

■ Legibility? The most legible color combinations, in order of visibility: black on yellow, green on white, red on white, blue on white, and black on white.

(*Magazine Design & Production*, 4551 W. 107th St., Overland Park, KS 66207)

Proofread the errors out of your publication

Proofreading may not be the most exciting or glamorous task in the world, but your publication's credibility depends on it. Successful proofreading is a team effort: the best method is to have several different people check your copy. If that's not possible — or if you just want to eliminate as many errors as you can before others look at your copy — you can still produce an error-free document by paying attention to these tips:

☐ **Make a line screen** that blocks out the page so that you can only look at one line at a time. This will slow you down and keep you from skimming just for content.

☐ **Read your document out of order.** Go backwards, page by page, line by line with our line screen, or word by word, or just shuffle the pages (make sure they've been numbered!). Again, this forces you to slow your pace and concentrate on individual words.

☐ **Look carefully at the beginning of everything.** Many people race straight into the main body of the document, glancing only briefly at the first few words of a new page, paragraph, or section.

☐ **Errors come in clusters.** Don't let yourself relax when you spot a typo, or you'll miss the one right next to it.

☐ **Be conscious of typeface changes.** A different typeface can distract you. Double check yourself by reading several times everything that's been underlined, CAPITALIZED, or printed in **bold** or *italics*.

☐ **Check numbering.** Make sure the chapters match the page numbers listed in your table of contents. Don't misnumber diagrams, figures, or tables, and don't skip any numbers.

☐ **Double check directions in the text.** If you read "see diagram on page 10," make sure the diagram is there on page 10. It may have been moved in a later version of the text.

☐ **Add up all numbers.** Are calculations in the copy correct? Watch out for misplaced commas and decimal points. Make sure columns of numbers are evenly aligned.

☐ **Do you have a bibliography?** Check your alphabetical order, then verify the spelling of all names and titles. Compare each entry with whatever style sheet you use for proper form, and look for errors in punctuation and spelling.

☐ **Vary your proofreading routine.** Proofread at a different time every day. If possible, take a break, put the document aside, and come back to it later with a rested eye. Reread the last few lines or pages to refresh your memory.

(*Simply Stated*, Document Design Center, 3333 K ST., Washington, DC 20007)

Good design can increase readership

The way a newsletter or magazine is designed tells much about whether it will be read or not. Here are three techniques you can use to increase readership:

- **Headlines** set in all capital letters are difficult to read.
- **Body copy** set in all capital letters is extremely difficult to read. Use upper and lower case type.
- **Reversed type** (white type on black background) is more difficult to read than type set black on white.

(*The Office Newsletter*, Lowen Publishing, P.O. Box 6870-432, Torrance, CA 90504)

Don't forget these rules

For good editorial layout here are four rules to follow:

1. Set headlines three times the body size; larger is acceptable — smaller is not.

2. A story without pictures has only the headline to sell it. Therefore make headlines interesting.

3. Mugshots need never be more than 1" by 1 1/2", that is, unless your job depends upon it.

4. Whoever makes a mugshot 20 picas wide and 30 picas deep should be in another business—like making Wanted posters for the post office.

(*80 Basic Rules for Good Editorial Layouts,* Ragan Communications, 212 W. Superior Street, Chicago, IL 60610)

When to redesign your publication

Redesign when you have a new editorial concept or change in focus, says Jan White, author and designer. Good design is driven by good editorial — the two elements should work together in a total communications package.

☐ **Redesign when your competition** forces you to look at yourself because they're better.

☐ **Redesign when your publishing** strategy dictates that your ad people need a new product to sell.

(*Mastering Graphics*, by Jan V. White)

Size of type determines ideal column width

If you use a desk-top system, remember: set type within the "readability range."

Readers can most easily read columns of type that are neither too narrow nor too wide: 39 lower case x's on a standard typewriter is an ideal. But, you can go up 50% or down 25% without loss of readers. If you use 10 or 11 point type, set your columns between 10 and 22 picas, and you'll be fine.

Lesson: The ideal width is a factor of type height.

(*Arnold's Ancient Axioms*, by Edmund Arnold)

Charts should be functional

The rules that govern the use of charts are no different from those governing other communication.

- ☐ **Simpler is almost always better:** two-dimensional lines and bars are easier to understand than 3-dimensional.
- ☐ **Beauty should serve function,** not the other way around: the purpose of color is to differentiate, not to please.

Remember: the purpose of a chart is to make numbers more easily understood.

Ten most common proofreading errors

If you know where most errors occur when proofreading, you'll increase your ability to catch *all* errors. Here's a breakdown of the most common errors:

Letters omitted	14.5%
Substitutions	14.1%
Space omitted	10.7%
Punctuation mark omitted	10.5%
Transpositions	6.6%
Word omitted	5.9%
Small letter for capital	2.9%
Full line omitted	1.7%
Spelling error	1.6%
Capital for small letter	1.1%

Studies have shown that mistakes are most likely in the latter half of a long line and in the middle of longer words. Pay special attention to the obvious (headlines, numbers) and the mundane (periods, commas, quotation marks).

(*Stet! Tricks of the Trade for Writers and Editors*, Editorial Experts, Inc., 85 S. Bragg St., Alexandria, VA 22312)

Give your newsletter some space

No more than half the space in a modern publication to a general audience should be occupied by body copy. *Why?* A dense page discourages readership, and if you don't have readers, you aren't communicating. So what do you put on the other half of the page?

- Large, thematic photos and clarifying art.
- Headlines, blurbs, and break-out quotes.
- White space around each column and to the outside of each page.

Spot more errors while proofreading

Read your copy backwards and then list the errors you spot over a month's time. Usually there's a pattern.

Remember: Scrutinize features that come in sets; brackets, parentheses, quotation marks, and dashes.

(*Currents,* Public Service Company of Oklahoma, Box 201, Tulsa, OK 74102)

A forceful technique

If you emphasize items in a series with bullets, follow the "Rule of Six": when you have more than six items, alternate between solid and hollow bullets.

By following this rule you will maintain the emphasizing technique, without squandering the force of the bullet through overuse.

(*Do-It-Yourself-Designer,* by Ray Dorn, 1013 S. Ahrens, Lombard, IL 60148)

Color it pretty, but don't overdo

If you use an attention-getting device (such as color) in your newsletter or other writings, remember the *Law of Diminishing Returns.* One device draws maximum attention. Two devices split your attention. Four or more devices lose their attention-getting effectiveness completely.

(*Eighty Basic Rules for Good Editorial Layouts,* by Ray Dorn)

Keep your reader reading

The subhead is the best way to break up columns of copy in a newsletter or report because it keys the next topic. **But remember:** The reader knows (subconsciously) that a break is coming at the beginning and end of each page and column, so don't put a sub-head where it isn't functional — at the top or bottom of a page.

Lesson: Keep subheads in the middle third of the column or page.

Easy to read publications

For a very legible publication Ed Arnold has the following suggestions:

• Use a standard Times Roman typeface when choosing your body copy. The finishing strokes form a baseline that keeps the eye moving easily and quickly. And the variance in the width of the stroke within the letter allows the reading eye to distinguish letters quickly.

• Use Helvetica for headlines.

(*Arnold's Ancient Axioms,* by Edmund Arnold)

PUBLISHING

Here we take the broad approach to questions, such as — Do we really need a publication at all? If so, what form should it take? How do we know if it is performing its function? Big budget or small, these hints can help you make the dollars go farther.

Plan your cover

When planning the cover of your magazine, newsletter, or newspaper, remember that every cover should:

- State the name of the publication.
- State the date, audience, and purpose of the publication.
- In a publication longer than four pages, highlight the most important stories.
- Establish the style of photography.
- Indicate the most important story in the publication.
- Persuade the reader that the entire issue is valuable.
- Make the reader want to read something in the issue immediately.
- Neither confuse nor distract.
- Reach out to the reader's self-interest.

How to name a newsletter

When naming a newsletter do so using the four Ws:
What: *New and Notes; Sporting Trends.*
When: *Perspective; Insight.*
Where: *Around the Plant; Memphis Insider.*
Who: *Good People; The Working Communicator.*

Survey questionnaire must be easy to complete

If conducting a survey, make sure your survey is easy to read and to complete.

☐ When providing a long list of choices, be sure to put a blank space after every 5th choice. This will make the questionnaire easier to fill out.

☐ Use a consistent presentation format. Use a vertical format and have all answers listed in a column, rather than across. Also, use one column of questions on a page instead of two columns on a page.

☐ List possible answers by using numbers rather than letters, lines or checkmarks. Respondents should be instructed to circle the appropriate number(s). This helps the data entry person who can simply enter the number directly rather than translate a letter or checkmark.

(Dale Paulson, President, Association Research Group, Alexandria, VA, writing in *Association Trends*, 4948 St. Elmo Ave., Bethesda, MD 20814)

Questions you must ask if starting a magazine

Magazines sometimes fail, not because they are of poor quality, but because many think that all you have to do is have an idea — and then start publishing. Here are seven questions to ask before starting a publication.

- **Is there a field?** Magazines exist because their audiences have an interest. Your magazine will succeed if the field is large enough in terms of circulation and/or advertising.

- **Can you develop editorial content to serve the field?** Successful magazines have good editorial content. Can you state the purpose of the magazine in ten words or less — and then lay out detailed editorial plans for a year's issues? Don't say to yourself, the magazine will "evolve over time." This is a sure sign of the editorial uncertainty that leads to failure.

- **How can you test the concept?** Virtually any concept can be tested. Testing is often done by conducting focus groups with potential readers. This research will help you avoid a disaster.

- **Is the magazine financially viable?** You might have a large, interested audience, but does it have enough to pay for subscriptions? Is there sufficient advertising?

- **Is the plan feasible?** A long-range plan is necessary. This plan must include concept, editorial approach, market for circulation, market for advertising, competition, time schedule.

- **Is there enough money?**

- **Do you possess the needed entrepreneurial characteristics?** Some entrepreneurial characteristics include: skills in long-range planning and fund-raising; attention to details; and persistence.

Focus on the customer

If your business involves publishing, newsletter publisher Al Goodloe suggests the following:

1. Call five subscribers a week; once a month, go to lunch with a subscriber.
2. Try focus groups. Get five or ten subscribers together.
3. Do frequent surveys of readers' interests, opinions, practices.
4. Attend the conferences and seminars where your readers gather.

(*Publishers Multinational Direct*, 174 E. 74th St., New York, NY 10021)

SPEECHES & PRESENTATIONS

From the simplest office talk about a new copy machine to a formal address about the national economy before a thousand listeners, the prepared communicator will get the message across (and the one who isn't prepared, won't). These suggestions may help you shine in the activity where everyone expects you to be an expert.

Link an unpopular idea to an acceptable one

Selling an unpopular idea or concept can be easier if you link it to something more palatable. A second idea will tend to "rub off" on the first. If you put two thoughts together, doing so makes them *seem* almost related (even if they aren't), and as your listener considers both of them, the less acceptable concept comes to seem more reasonable. For instance, to secure support for an expensive project, you might say: "This may cost us a lot, but it's okay to think about spending money if we're going to make money in the end."

(*Tips & Tactics*, PR Publishing Company, Inc., Dudley House, P.O. Box 600, Exeter, NH 03833)

Research your audience

If you're about to give a speech, research your audience and the room in which you are scheduled to speak. It's important to know if you're lecturing before a group of 15 or 115.

If you're speaking in front of a small group, you'll be able to be less formal by using charts, an easel, and magic marker. For larger groups you'll need amplifying equipment and perhaps a lectern, carousel projector and screen.

(*50 Rules to Keep a Client Happy*, by Fred Poppe; Harper & Row, Publishers, Inc., 10 East 53rd St., New York, NY 10022)

How to become a speechwriter

Speechwriter Tim Koranda of the New York Power Authority recently offered tips on how to become a speechwriter:

☐ Speechwriting is not an entry level position. You first have to learn about writing and the world. Getting a shot at writing a speech usually occurs by accident.

☐ You should be a person who is curious. You should look for patterns in events. Since speechwriting is a solitary profession, you must be happy being solitary.

☐ Read a lot. To begin with, you have to keep up with the business and the trade papers; you have to know what's going on in your industry. You might also read poetry since it helps in writing for the ear.

☐ Volunteer your talents for a local politician. You won't get paid, but you'll get experience and exposure.

Speeches are a powerful form of communication

Consider the speeches of the Rev. Jesse Jackson, Gov. Mario Cuomo, or Martin Luther King, Jr. Speechwriting expert Jerry Tarver has these suggestions:

1. Limit your scope. Don't try to do too much in a single speech. Pick a simple idea and develop it fully.

2. Make an ugly outline. The outline is a tool. Don't expect the first outline always to be the final one. Feel free to play around with different approaches. If your first outline is too neat and pretty, you may be reluctant to alter it.

3. Don't jump into the subject. Most speeches require thirty seconds to three minutes of introductory material before the subject is broached directly. Most audiences are not ready to listen to the main ideas of a speech until they've had a minute or so to get adjusted to the speaker.

4. Use transitions. Speeches need strong transitions between ideas to help listeners keep up. Use such phrases as "turning now," "let's next examine," or "so much for costs, but what about income?"

5. Tell stories. Don't rely only on statistics, quotes, and examples to make your points. Occasionally develop an illustration for about half a minute. Stories hold attention and give variety to the support for your ideas.

Write and give better speeches

In a speech, the strongest idea in a sentence should be saved for the end, and the punch should come not from a negative idea, but from a positive one. Inverting John F. Kennedy's famous line, for example, emasculates it: "Ask what you can do for your country, ask not what your country can do for you." The words on the page mean the same thing as the original, but if you speak it, the message drops off a cliff.

Your message will be loud and clear if you end your sentences, your paragraphs, and your speech with a positive statement.

(Dr. Jerry Tarver, speechwriting expert)

Where to get publicity

If you write or give speeches, send your best work to *Vital Speeches of the Day* (c/o City News Publishing Co., Box 606, Southold, NY 11971), or *Speechwriter's Newsletter* (212 W. Superior Street, Chicago, IL 60610) where it might be reprinted for a larger audience.

Don't let them sleep

When you show slides at a meeting, darken the room only as much as necessary. Few slides need a totally darkened room, which often depresses the spirit and encourages slumber, not to mention inhibiting the give-and-take that is usually desirable in a successful presentation.

Just the facts for your speech
Once you've found your topic, the most important thing in a speech is to narrow your focus. Too many presenters think they have to tell everything they know about a subject. In fact, don't try to make more than four points in a speech. Three is ideal. and give just the facts that are necessary. The more you put your speech in focus, the clearer it will be to your audience.

(*What's Your Point?* by Bob Boylan, Point Publications, 3701 Shoreline Drive, Suite 106, Wayzata, MN 55391)

When writing a speech, repeat, repeat, repeat
One key to a good speech is repetition, or *anaphora,* "the deliberate repetition of a word or phrase at the beginning of several successive clauses." Two famous examples are Martin Luther King's "I have a dream" speech and Churchill's exhorting the British against the Nazis: "...we shall fight on the beaches, we shall fight in the fields and in the streets, we shall fight in the hills; we shall never surrender...."

Use anaphora when you write a speech, and you just might move nations.

Present tense draws a crowd
A speech is much more gripping if it's filled with present-tense constructions, rather than flat statements of what "was" or what you "did." Couching things in the here-and-now will communicate action and involvement on your part, and that allows your audience to feel active and involved right along with you.

(Jim Ylisela, editor of *The Hispanic Times,* and speechwriter, 550 West Arlington, Suite 710, Chicago, IL 60614)

Make your trips relaxing and more successful
To air travelers who are upset by carry-on luggage restrictions:

• **Pack less,** and color coordinate clothes to eliminate extras. Remember, many hotels now supply shampoos, hair dryers, robes.

• **Ship ahead** extra clothes by UPS air service. The shipment may cost about $16 and is guaranteed to arrive.

• **Reserve** a smoking-area seat or one immediately in front of the smokers' section. That way, you'll be among the first to enter the plane and will have more room to scrunch your carry-ons in better spaces.

• **Arrive early** to make sure your bags make the plane. Put your name on the outside and inside of your luggage. Be sure that the ticket agent puts the proper destination stickers on your bags. And be sure to keep your baggage stubs, without which you won't be able to file a claim.

(*Successful Meetings,* $5 a copy; Bill Communications, Inc., 633 Third Ave., New York, NY 10017)

Speech rehearsal

When rehearsing a speech, tape and retain each second or third run-through, suggests Andy Markens, of Markens Communications Incs., Palo Alto, California. When you listen to yourself, you'll be motivated by your improvements—and your weaknesses will be easier to spot.

Visual aids: Get the most impact

To get the most impact from visual aids at meetings, follow these tips:
- Don't show a visual aid until the exact moment you plan to discuss it.
- When you do reveal it, give the audience a few seconds to take in the information before discussing it.
- Make one point per visual, with minimal and readable text.
- Sometimes a slide is complicated. Offer guidance and take the time to point out its details.
- Point only to the visual to clarify—otherwise focus on the audience. You'll give the impression that you know your stuff.
- Be creative. Do the unexpected. *Some ideas:* Use a live model, or members of your audience as visual aids.

(*Successful Meetings*)

Become a polished, professional speaker

To make sure that your next speech will go off without a hitch, write your own introduction. That way, you'll make sure that it's accurate. It will also strike the tone you seek. Most chairpeople will not object. A few more ideas:

■ Take a half-minute to organize yourself at the lectern. Look up and make eye contact before you begin. You'll feel in control, and you'll *be* in control.

■ After you begin, don't be afraid to move away from the lectern. You'll look more relaxed and you'll avoid the temptation to hang on to the lectern as if it might get away from you.

■ If you use visual aids, dim the room. Darkening it entirely might lead to slumber.

■ Don't rely on visual aids as a crutch. They are a side-show, not the show itself.

■ Give handouts at the end of the meeting, not the beginning. Otherwise the audience will be distracted by the handouts while you're speaking.

■ Never end a question-and-answer session with "I don't know." Your presentation should end on an upbeat note.

("You as the Speaker," by Maria A. Lenoir in *The Meeting Manager*, 1950 Stemmons Freeway, Dallas, TX 75207)

Conduct Q & A sessions at the end of a speech
If you are called upon to make a speech, try wrapping it up with a question and answer session. Here are a few Q & A tips:
- ☐ **Always repeat the question.** This is helpful to your audience and it buys you time.
- ☐ **Watch your body language.** Avoid defensive postures. As you listen to the question, pause, lean forward, smile, and answer consisely.
- ☐ **Break away from the questioner** when he or she has finished. Address your answer to the entire audience (thus preventing "ping-pong" exchanges).
- ☐ **Stick to what you know.**
- ☐ **Pass the buck.** If you must dodge a question, bounce it to an authority in the audience.

Be a better writer, speaker
Roger Ailes, who counseled President Ronald Reagan during the Mondale/Reagan Debates, offers this advice: If you give speeches in public, keep in your wallet an index card and list the key phrases of 10 stories that will entertain audiences for the next 10 years. *Why?* Because rarely will you speak to the same audience twice.

(*You are the Message, Secrets of the Master Communicators*, by Roger Ailes; Dow Jones-Irwin, Homewood, IL 60430)

Keep trying to get publicity
To increase your publicity, send your speech clips to radio stations. The smaller radio stations, especially, are hungry for material. Routinely send them tapes with short bits from your better speeches.

(Manny Goldman, 517 S. Jefferson St., Chicago, IL 60607)

Know the type of speech your audience requires
Speeches given at different times of the day should sound different.
- **Breakfast meetings require brevity.** Remember that your audience has awakened an hour or two earlier than usual—and they still face a day of work. Be merciful; be brief.
- **A mid-afternoon panel presentation requires flexibility.** Since panel presentations run notoriously long, the last person may find time squeezed. Be prepared to shorten your presentation.
- **An after-banquet speech will find your audience in a good mood,** presumably after several hours of drinking. Don't ruin the mood with a speech too serious—or too long.

(*Executive Communications*, Magna Publications, Inc., 2718 Dryden Drive, Madison, WI 53704-3006)

End your speech with an idea
Kill that "Thank you." A tag line to signal the end of a speech is the coward's way out. If you really want to thank an audience, two words won't do the trick. Better to end a speech with an idea than a crutch.

(*Your Next Speech: 66 Ways to Improve It* by Jerry Tarver)

The correct way to use visuals
When using a visual aid, don't talk *to* it. Rather, talk to the audience as much as possible. This, of course, is difficult if you are talking while writing or reading. If this is the case, turn partially toward the audience or else don't talk and write at the same time.

(*Cincinnati Bell Magazine*, 201 East Fourth St., Cincinnati, OH 45201)

Don't close with a quote
Avoid ending a speech with a quote. It sounds pretentious. Besides, you want your audience to remember *your* ideas, not someone's who died 200 years ago. Instead, restate your main points, or end on a lighter note, with a story or joke of your own creation.

(Willis Foss, 400 Glenway, Amherst, VA 24251)

Be a better leader: confident not charismatic
To be a good meeting leader you don't have to be charismatic. But you do need *stage presence.*

When you begin the meeting, walk into the room with calm confidence, proceed to the leader's chair, arrange papers and notes, and then turn to the group *as the leader.*

■ **Open with a brief statement** of the purpose of the meeting. *And don't make this common error:* opening the meeting with a long statement that rambles on and on and on. Your statement should be short and to the point. And never express your opinions in the opening statement or participants will think they're there only to approve your ideas.

■ **Always do your homework** or you'll lose control of the meeting. You should:
1. *Know* the audience
2. *Anticipate* meeting attitudes and positions
3. *Speak* the language of the participants
4. *Consider* the suggestions and opinions of everyone
5. *Avoid* distracting mannerisms (like playing with a pencil while talking)
6. And always *control* the meeting, never let it slip away.

(*How to Run Better Business Meetings, A reference guide for managers*, by the 3M Meeting Management Team, McGraw-Hill Book Co.; $18.95)

Improve your lectures

Lectures are often dull, but they are necessary at times. To keep your lectures from being unnecessarily dull:

- **Role-play.** Choose an audience member to help you act out a situation. Doing this gets your participants involved and makes it easier to explain abstract theories.
- **Go "stereophonic."** Have two leaders take turns talking at frequent intervals. This, like the half-hour TV show, gives the audience refreshing breaks.
- **Plant key questions.** Tell a few audience members what you want them to ask—others will follow suit and enliven your lecture.

(*25 Ways to Improve Any Lecture* by Sivasailam Thiagarjan)

Use humor to control your audience

If you want to control your audience while speaking, use humor. Speakers who can make their audiences laugh are in control of their audiences.

The safest kind of humor is the historical anecdote that is (1) funny but (2) also makes a point. *Why?* Because if the humor falls flat, you still can salvage the point—and the audience will never know you expected a laugh.

(*Capital Ideas for Speechwriters* by Jim Sellers, 1730 Minda Drive, Eugene, OR 97401)

When speaking, demand the props you want

Never be hesitant to ask for the type of microphone or lectern you feel most comfortable with. In fact, Joe Friedman, from Executive Technique in Chicago, says you must *demand* what you want. After all, you're going to give the speech.

(The First Annual Speechwriter's Conference in Chicago)

Praise the audience

Everybody likes compliments, so a sure way for speakers to warm up audience members is to find out about one of their recent accomplishments—a successful fund-raising project, a worthwhile community project, increased sales, an industry award, etc.,—and praise them for it. Be sure to provide enough details to show that you have done your homework.

Tips on using microphones and notecards

Free yourself from the podium with a pendant microphone that hangs around your neck, but don't use that freedom to start pacing back and forth, or it's possible you'll distract your audience. If you use notecards when giving a speech, try using bigger notecards that hold more information and don't need to be switched over very frequently. Remember to number the cards in case you drop them.

(*Prism*, IABC/Chicago, 203 N. Wabash, Chicago, IL 60601)

'Aha! Now I see what she means.'

Visual aids can bring your presentation to life if you use them correctly. Carolyn Dickson, president of Voice-Pro Associates, says that a visual aid is effective when it "replaces a verbal description and makes listeners say 'A-ha! Now I see what she means.'" Other hints for visual aid use include:

- <u>Stay simple.</u> Remember, your audience has to listen to you at the same time they're studying the visual aid.
- <u>Make sure people can see and read easily.</u> Are your numbers and letters large enough? Also, different colors can make charts and graphs easier to focus on.
- <u>Don't use slides</u> If you expect your audience to take notes. They won't be able to when the lights are off for the projector.
- <u>Remember your audience.</u> Talk to your listeners, not to the visual aid.

(*BFG Today*, 3925 Embassy Parkway, Akron, OH 44313-1799)

Memorize your speeches

Holding notes during speeches can be awkward. Why not try memorizing a speech? The ideal speech to memorize is a short, important speech like a dedication or award ceremony.

1. **Memorize the form of the speech,** not the words. Memorize how it is structured, and how it flows from one idea to the next.

2. **Memorize a passage at a time.** Read the speech aloud several times, and try to visualize how each passage fits into the whole speech.

3. **If you forget or go blank,** don't panic—and don't try to recall the exact word that you forgot. Instead, speak extemporaneously along the general topic.

(*Handbook for Public Relations Writing* by Thomas Bivins)

Hold on to your audience with these techniques

How many presentations have you attended where the speaker lost the audience within minutes? Were you the speaker? Watch for the signs that your audience is losing interest; then, draw them back with a few simple techniques:

- ■ **Talking.** When audience members are talking, they aren't listening to you. *Pause.* The silence will draw attention back to you.

- ■ **Confusion.** Do people look puzzled? You're talking over their heads. *Use plain English.* Avoid technical jargon, and recap after any difficult points: "In a nutshell, this means..."

- ■ **Inattention.** Your audience may be unable to hear you. *Check your volume.* Turn up your microphone, or speak louder and more clearly.

- ■ **Fatigue.** Are people stifling yawns, rubbing their eyes, or gazing blankly into space? *Take a break.* After a few minutes' rest, your audience will return refreshed and attentive.

(*NewsClips*, Quill Corporation, Lincolnshire, IL)

Stand to the left for slide presentations

When making a slide presentation, always stand so that the audience will see you to the *left* of the screen. Focus-group research has shown that his position will be most effective for you.

(*Communication World/* IABC, One Hallidie Plaza, Suite 600, San Francisco, CA 94201)

Rules for a quick thank-you speech

You can give a sincere and effective thank-you speech in less than one minute with the help of Grant Gard, author of *The Art of Public Speaking.* Just follow four rules:

☐ Express your gratitude: "This award is an honor and a privilege for me to receive."
☐ Acknowledge and thank people who helped: "My staff worked many long hours on this project," or "I couldn't have achieved this without the help of my friend and mentor, Joe Smith."
☐ Tell what you'll do with the award: "I'll be placing this plaque in my reception area where my staff and I can take pride in our accomplishment," or "I plan to donate this money to the college scholarship fund."
☐ Two more words: "Thank you."

Tips for good public speaking

Public speaking, for managers, is a part of the job. Before a speech, practice in front of a mirror: tape record your presentation, play it back, listen to yourself, and ask, "Would I be bored by this speech?" If you answer yes, change your speech and try again.

When giving a speech, good public speakers agree on these suggestions:

- **Stride confidently** to the lectern and stand tall, with your weight evenly distributed on both feet. The best speakers will carry index cards to the lectern, having a word or phrase printed on each one, reminding the speaker of the points he or she wants to cover.

- **Put your hands by your side,** and don't be afraid to use them. The inexperienced speaker will be self-conscious about his or her hands.

- **Don't use corporate lingo,** or technical references that your listeners won't understand. Technical language will put your listener to sleep. Always try to tell it in layman's terms.

- **Use humor.** Make people laugh. But do it at your own expense rather than ridiculing others.

(Adapted in part from *MW*, Administrative Management Society, AMS Building, 2360 Maryland Road, Willow Grove, PA 19090.)

SUPPLIERS

No communicator can do the job without the help of suppliers, most of whom are outside the organization. Choosing and handling them presents pitfalls you may not have considered; consider them now with this guidance.

Hiring a consultant

Don't just hurriedly hire a consultant without asking yourself some questions:
1. Why am I hiring a consultant at this specific time?
2. Can I accept strong advice?
3. Can I find the consultant through business friends?
4. Can I hire a peer?
5. Will I hire someone I dislike if he or she knows how to solve my problems?
6. Is industry experience important?

(*First and Last*, William Dunk Partners, P.O. Box 7402, Greenwich, CT 06836-7402)

Get more from freelancers

The first phone call to a freelancer can pave the way for an assignment done to your mutual satisfaction — if handled properly.
- Be thorough: discuss deadline, type of piece, length, fee.
- Be up front: don't decide on a 2,500-word story at a stated price, and then ask for sidebars and captions later.
- Determine the compatibility — if any — of your computer systems.

(*The Maranto Memo*, Maranto Communications, P.O. Box 429, Wilton, CT 06897)

How to choose a printing company

Choosing a printing company involves more than just looking at samples. Peggy Fernandez, production manager for Vision Marketing, evaluates printers with this step-by-step process:

In your initial contact with a representative, find out what kinds of printing the company does, what types of equipment it uses, and the sort of products it typically produces. Request samples and an equipment list.

If the samples are satisfactory, meet with the rep and get three references. Check them.

Give the "5P" test: Plant, Personnel, Products, Printing Processes, and Paper. The rep should be well-informed on all of these topics.

Get a bid from the company on at least three prospective jobs. This will help you evaluate three things: how the company interprets your specifications; whether they can suggest greater efficiency regarding press and/or paper; and their promptness in returning a quote to you.

"If all this seems long and tedious, it is," says Fernandez. "However, it works."

(*Blue Line*, Northern California Print Center, 665 Third St., San Francisco, CA 94107)

Lower your publishing costs

No editor likes working on a meager budget, but just about every editor's boss likes saving money. Here are two ideas on how to lower publishing costs while you safeguard quality:

☐ **Create** an instrument to help you determine your revenue and expenses each month. Ask your accounting department, budget section, or comptroller for help in creating a cost analysis tool so that all you need to do each month is write in some figures and do a little math. This will help you adjust priorities and accurately identify areas where cuts can be made.

☐ **Think** about your use of four-color and black-and-white reproductions. What about decreasing the amount of four-color work and opting for better black-and-white pictures and line art that can compete with four-color subjects? Can you replace four-color work with two-color work? Both can save money in production costs.

If you account for every penny spent producing a quality publication at a reasonable cost, the "powers that be" may well consider your department for expansion first when planning next year's budget.

Save money: ask printer important question

When you are having a folder, brochure, or any kind of printing done, ask the printer how the job will "cut to waste." That means: How much blank paper will be cut off the sheet after the printing is done — such trim can be used for note pads, telephone-call memos, etc.

Sure way to bundle bulk mail

If you use string or cord to bundle envelopes for bulk mailing, lay the cord in an empty envelope box, running across the narrow dimension, and with both ends draped over the sides of the box.

When the box is full, or partially full, it's easy to tie the cord with no danger of the envelopes slipping out of your fingers.

Listen for the word 'No'

When looking for a printer, listen to what the printing company's sales reps *don't* tell you. Advice from Lee Zierten, of Bradley Printing Company: "Does he or she ever say 'No' to you? Avoid giving you any bad news? Blames problems on people at the plant, the designer, the paper, humidity, or the ink rather than saying 'It's my fault' when a job doesn't turn out the way you want it? If so, you'd be better off with another sales representative and another printer." In other words, if the sales rep says, "Yes, we can do that," to every request, take it with a grain of salt — if you take it at all.

(*Ury News*, Bernard E. Ury & Associates, 307 N. Michigan Avenue, Chicago, IL 60601)

TELEPHONE USE

Next to the typewriter (or word processor), the telephone is essential for the professional communicator. Yet not all of us know how to use the phone efficiently, so that it will help us get the job done and won't get in our way. These tips can make your day a little smoother.

Your most important asset is the customer

Are the people answering phones representing your company fairly? Sometimes in the rush of a day's work we forget that the customer is the most important asset of a business. Here are five changes to make when talking over the phone.

Instead of: Let me ask you a question.
Use: May I ask you a question, or Do you mind if I ask you some questions?

Instead of: She isn't back from lunch yet.
Use: She's away from her desk, but I expect her soon.

Instead of: He's on his coffee break.
Use: He's away from his desk, how can I help you?

Instead of: He's not here.
Use: He's unavailable at the moment, how can I help you?

Instead of: I don't know, we don't handle that.
Use: Sorry, I can't answer (or help you with) that, but I can refer you to someone who can.

Quit thumbing through your rolodex

Are you constantly looking for the same telephone number in the phone book or flipping through your rolodex even though you have dialed that number many times? The best thing to do when memory fails is to write down the numbers you use most often and then tape that list to the base of your phone.

Can you answer "Yes!" to these questions?

If you have heavy phone contact with your company's customers, be able to answer these questions "Yes!":

- **Do you answer** the phone before the second ring?

- **When you transfer** a call, do you tell the caller the extension number in case you get disconnected?

- **When you promise** to follow up on something, do you start as soon as you hang up? If not, do you write a note to yourself immediately so you won't forget?

- **Do you help** callers reach the right people if you don't have the information they need?

(*Helmsman*, USF&G, P.O. Box 1138, Baltimore, MD 21203)

Don't waste valuable time

If someone is wasting your time by talking endlessly over the phone, here's a way of ending the call: Knock loudly on your desk top and say, "Somebody's at my door. I'll talk to you later."

(*Professional Business Communications*)

Try these practical telephone tips

☐ If you use note cards or a rolodex to record names, addresses, and phone numbers, be sure to write the phone number at the very top of the card. This will save you from having to pull the card out or lean way over when you need the number in a hurry.

☐ When you're leaving a message on an answering machine, state your phone number not once, but twice. That way, the listener won't have to rewind to get part of it. Even if the person does get the number down all at once, the repetition gives a chance to confirm that the number is correct.

☐ Take notes during every telephone conversation. Make this an automatic reflex. Note taking will focus your thoughts on the conversation. Also, whether or not you end up doing business with the caller, you may need to remember or repeat information from the phone call in order to make a decision, or justify one.

☐ New job? Tape your new company's address and phone number to your telephone for easy reference until you've got it memorized. Also, tape one or two important numbers to the handle of your phone. Instead of looking them up every time, you can pick up the phone and just start dialing.

Put the radio on hold

Don't sentence your telephone callers to empty silence or elevator music when you put them on hold. Install a system that will allow them to listen to a local news station while they're waiting to be connected. Your callers will enjoy listening to an informative program instead of counting the passing seconds and being bored.

Build instant rapport on the telephone

When your work requires heavy phone contact, remember that you can establish rapport with your voice alone. Just adjust your tone of voice and your speaking tempo to match the person on the other end of the line. If Mr. Smith from New York speaks rapidly in a high-pitched tone, don't respond with a lazy drawl. Match his speed and pitch, and Mr. Smith will feel he's talking to someone he can trust, someone who understands him. Chances are he won't even notice that you're "mimicking" him.

(Genie Z. Laborde, *Influencing with Integrity*, Symtomy Publishing, Palo Alto, CA)

Identify yourself as you speak
It's helpful to those on the other end of a speakerphone conversation if you make a habit of introducing everyone in the room at the outset of each call. Also, urge your colleagues to identify themselves each time they speak.

(Mel Sorenson, Fulco, Inc., 136 East Main St., Denville, NJ 07834)

Get down to business
Long-winded callers are notorious time-wasters. Here's an effective tip for dealing with repeat offenders: Announce you're putting your secretary on the line to take notes, so that you can listen more attentively. It's guaranteed to prevent official business from segueing into an account of last week's fishing trip — particularly if you remind your caller of the third party on the line.

Use the power of telephones
A survey firm recently phoned 5,000 companies that had taken out $200-a-month ads in the Yellow pages. The majority of these companies failed to ask the caller's name, and failed to recognize the call as a sales opportunity.

If your company has spent hundreds of dollars on advertising, teach employees how to use the phone.

(*Illinois Economic Report*, 620 E. Adams St., Lower Level, Springfield, IL 62701)

Plan your long-distance calls in advance
To keep your long-distance phone charges to a minimum, plan your calls in advance. Make a list of items you want to discuss, and stick to it without taking time out to chat. If the person you're calling is out, leave as precise a message as you can. That will give your colleague a head start on helping you before returning the call.

(*Carolina Lines*, Southern Bell Telephone & Telegraph, P.O. Box 752, Columbia, SC 29202)

Answer the phone call on the first ring
Brenda Tippets answered 37,000 calls this way and increased her company's sales.

"I believe more sales are won or lost on the other end of the telephone than by anything else in our business," says Vice Chairman of Eastman Kodak Co., Phillip Samper.

(*Customer Service Newsletter*, Customer Equipment Service Dispatcher, 8701 Georgia Ave., Silver Spring, MD 20910)

If you must say no, try the sandwich technique

When your answer to a customer's request must be "no," make sure you maintain a positive image for yourself and the company. *How do you do this?* Try the sandwich technique — sandwich the "no" between two "yes's":

- ☐ **First, be positive.** Thank the caller for the request and let the caller know you will do everything you can to help.
- ☐ **Be honest and specific.** If it isn't in your company policy to comply with the caller's request, explain that and offer your assistance another way.
- ☐ **End the conversation on a positive note.** "I'm happy to help you." Or "I hope I can be of assistance in the future."

Warning: Transferring an angry caller from one person to another only exacerbates the problem. This kind of response says the company is unwilling to give service.

Remember: When transferring calls, the chance of disconnecting callers increases — so give the caller the direct number before transferring.

Appease the grouchy caller

When dealing with an upset caller, make notes and tell the caller you are doing so. This will show him or her that you're interested in what he or she has to say.

(*Pulse*, Bethany Medical Center, Kansas City, KS 66102)

Hearing Aid

The next time you have trouble hearing someone over the phone, place your hand over the mouthpiece. This will make the voice on the other end clearer and louder.

(*The MDSS No-Name Newsletter*, P.O. 30037, Lansing, MI 48909)

Dealing with angry callers

When the voice on the other end of the line turns nasty:

- **Listen** carefully. Sometimes, that's all the caller wants.
- **Pause** for the count of two before you respond. Never interrupt.
- **To get** the caller speaking in a rational manner, ask questions that require more than a yes or no answer.
- **If anger** turns to abuse, say, "We really want to resolve this quickly. It would help if we could just focus on solving your problem."
- **Express** regret, apologize for inconvenience, but never say, "I'm sorry." That admission of guilt can lead to renewed attacks.
- **Avoid** the attack word "you." Instead, say, "I would recommend," or "May I suggest. . . ."

Get the most from your answering machine

Probably a third of the people who call you hang up the phone without leaving a message if they are greeted by an answering machine. *Why?* People are uncomfortable when talking to a machine. Make it easier for customers to talk into your machine by following these few rules:

- Keep the message short and simple. Most people, particularly business people, will feel that you're wasting their time if your message is long and involved.
- Don't try to be cute, clever, or funny.
- Ask callers for specific information, like what time they called. This will give them a "formula" to follow.
- Return calls as soon as possible. People will quit leaving messages if they realize their calls are never returned.

(*Field Talk*, Equitable Reserve Association, 116 S. Commercial St., Neenah, WI 54956)

Your telephone voice is your calling card

William Rush, voice consultant, says, "On the phone, voices are the number one means of assessing someone. Your telephone voice tells people about your interest, enthusiasm, credibility and, to some degree, signals your integrity.

To find out how you sound to others on the telephone, record your voice on tape. Speak extemporaneously — pretend you're making arrangements for a meeting or tell about last year's vacation. Play back the tape and objectively evaluate the quality of your telephone voice by asking yourself the following questions:

1. Are you like most people who tend to talk at a lower pitch on the phone? If so, concentrate on bringing your voice back up to your normal speaking pitch.

2. Does it sound as if you are mumbling? Be especially aware of how you sound when you are using a car phone, speaker phone, or portable phone.

3. Do you make most calls from a people-filled open room? Try to speak in a normal conversational tone to ensure that your message will be heard clearly.

4. Do you seem to fumble for words and thoughts when you speak extemporaneously? If you have an important call to make, decide beforehand what you need to say and what the other person needs to hear. When making a request, be direct. The more tentative-sounding the statement, the less likely the request will be granted.

5. Do you pepper your conversations with "uhs" and "umms" and "you knows?" To eliminate these distractions, pause each time you catch yourself saying them.

(*Halls Voice Improvement Program*, 500 N. Michigan Ave., Chicago, IL 60611. Send for a free brochure.)

Never put a client on hold
When calling a client, never have your secretary call for you.
Remember: You're supposed to make your client feel important, not yourself.

(*50 Rules To Keep A Client Happy* by Fred Poppe, Harper & Row Publishers)

Spend one hour making calls
To save valuable time, don't make phone calls until a certain time in the day. During that time, spend *only one hour* making the calls. The telephone — although extremely valuable — can waste time if used excessively. So the next time you reach for the phone, jot down the person's number you're about to call, and call him or her at your allotted time.

(*How to Organize Your Work and Your Life* by Robert Moskowitz, Doubleday & Company, Inc.)

Small courtesy saves trouble
When transferring a phone call, give the caller the name, title, division, and extension number of where you're transferring the call. If there is a disconnection, the caller will now know whom to call directly.

Use FX line instead of toll-free
Convenience is a major factor when people decide to patronize a business — especially when children, animals, senior citizens, or repeat visits are involved. So how does a business go about finding customers *outside* of its local area?

One way of attracting customers is to *not* use a toll-free number. Why? An 800 number connotes great distances, and most marketers want to create just the opposite impression.

A Foreign Exchange line (FX) might help attract customers outside your local area because it gives the impression that you're close and the phone calls are free. *The way it works:* The FX phone line is set up in the area you're trying to attract customers from, which means the phone number for that line is *local*, giving the impression that you're a local business, too. (Once they call, however, it's your job to get them into your store ... or to try your product.)

(*The Practice Builder*, The Evergreen Group, 2061 Business Center Dr., #107, Irvine, CA 92715)

Answering machines
Do away with wordy instructions on how to leave a message. Don't state the obvious. **An example of what to say:** "You've reached Doe's consulting firm; please leave a message and I'll get back to you."

Don't change your voice

Are you one of those people who tend to talk at a lower pitch while on the telephone? If so, don't. It sounds phony and pretentious — and no one will take you seriously. Concentrate on bringing your voice back up to your normal speaking pitch.

For a free brochure on speaking effectively, write *Halls Voice Improvement Program*, 500 N. Michigan Ave., Chicago, IL 60611. William Rush is spokesperson for *Halls*.

Hanging up

Always let the other person hang up the phone first. Then you won't be in danger of hanging up if he or she thinks of one last thing to say.

(Management Solutions)

TIME MANAGEMENT

Just not enough hours in the work day? There are a lot of ways to cram sixty seconds into the unforgiving minute; some of these may not have occurred to you. Look 'em over.

Do it right the first time, you will *save* time

A quality attitude is "do it right the first time," says Henry Jamroz of the Wayne County Department of Social Services. "Undoing it takes three times the effort and also frustrates and angers clients and staff. The old question still applies: 'Why is it you don't have time to do it right the first time, but you always can find time to do it over?'"

(Casewatch, cited in *MDSS No-Name Newsletter*, P.O. Box 30037, Lansing, MI 48909)

Look at caffeine if you're anxious and tense

The amount of caffeine in four cups of coffee is enough to substantially increase your anxiety level as well as your blood pressure. Caffeine can increase feelings of restlessness, nervousness, and panic. Don't forget that it's found not only in coffee, but also in tea, cola, and chocolate.

(Riverviews, 624 N. 4th St., Burlington, IA 52601)

Long memos: Stamp them out

Make a stamp that reads *Memo-Busters* and have managers stamp and return correspondence that was unnecessary, too lengthy, or sent to too many people.

Remember: The best way to cut down on long memos is to eliminate wordy phrases.

(The Main Ingredient, 120 W. Palatine Rd., Wheeling, IL 60090)

Business cards: Another way

Just handing out a business card is about as personal — and as memorable — as a handshake. If "I value your acquaintance" is the message you want to send, take the time to jot down your home phone number or office hours on your card as you hand it over. This show of concern is much more effective than having the information preprinted on the card. And recipients will be much more likely to hang on to information they can't easily get elsewhere.

(Joseph Remer, Insurance salesman, 160 3rd St. S., Winsted, MN 55395)

Write more effectively, efficiently

Some writing tasks are easy to complete quickly; others can be as tedious and time-consuming as painting the white line down the middle of a deserted highway. As a writer, you need to be able to manage your time as efficiently as any CEO. These strategies can help:

☐ **Recognize your priorities.**
List your writing tasks under categories of high, medium, and low payoff. Schedule your day so you can devote maximum time to tasks that reflect best on you and your company. Work on lower-ranking chores at other times.

☐ **Use your prime time.**
Tackle your most important writing tasks during "prime time" — your most ambitious and creative hours. 90 minutes when you feel fresh and full of energy can be worth three hours of trying to write when you're tired or distracted.

☐ **Don't reinvent the wheel.**
Use copies of press releases for reference when you need to write press releases of your own. Don't try to recreate each memo like a separate work of art.

☐ **Don't be a perfectionist.**
Not all projects deserve the amount of time your best efforts require. Don't spend as long on a memo explaining the company parking policy as you would on producing the company's annual report.

☐ **Get something on paper.**
Even when what you're writing sounds terrible to you, keep going. Rewriting a poor report is a lot easier than starting over.

☐ **Reward yourself.**
Treat yourself to a nice dinner, a good book, or a bottle of beer to celebrate when you finish an important project.

(Pat Roessle Materka, writing in *How to Improve Your Creativity*, published by The Council for the Advancement and Support of Education, 11 Dupont Circle, Suite 400, Washington, DC 20036)

Three ways to manage your writing time

Do you find yourself spending too much time writing, and not getting much written? Here are three tips from writing specialists on how to get the most out of your writing time:

- ■ Set aside a block of time. If you have three weeks to finish a report that will take six to eight hours to write, don't work on it fifteen minutes twice a day for three weeks. It's more efficient to find a five-hour stretch when you can write without interruption. At the end of that time, you will have a "zero-draft," which you can rewrite section by section in small blocks of time over the ensuing weeks.

(Peter Drucker in "How to Manage Your Time," *Harpers*)

- ■ Stop in the middle. If you can't finish a complete draft of a report in one sitting, it's better to stop writing in the middle of a paragraph than to try to finish a particular section or thought. It will be fairly easy to finish the thought the next day, and this writing will prime the pump for the next thought.

(Herbert Popper in "Six Guidelines for Fast, Functional Writing," *Chemical Engineering*)

- ■ Review with your purpose in mind. As the first step in rewriting, pick up each page of your draft, skim it, and ask yourself how the material on that page fulfills the report's objective. This process will quickly allow you to delete, add, change, and rearrange your material.

(Vincent Vici in "Ten Report Writing Pitfalls: How to Avoid Them," *Chemical Engineering*)

Advertise on business cards

Offers a discount on the back of your business card. If you're in the business of selling, always remember to give a business card to everyone you meet.

Another thing to remember: Most service organizations don't get letters of praise. If you're impressed with a service business (cleaners, limousine service, car wash, etc.), write them a letter and enclose your business card. Chances are the owner will post the letter and give you free publicity.

(Adapted in part from *The Art of Selling* by Tom Hopkins.)

Respond quickly to your mail

Much of the mail you get deserves a reply. You don't, however, need to follow up everything with another letter. Keep an eye out for mail to which you can respond with a couple of quick notes in the margin, then send back. It's an easy way to clarify your reply, and saves time as well. *Added benefit:* Writing notes in the margin communicates that the correspondence is "over," thus stemming the tide of paper across your desk.

Go through those bulging files

Do you have material in your files dating back to the Eisenhower administration? Ask yourself these questions when reviewing documents:

- **Is the information current?** Old or outdated materials can take up space better used for up-to-date facts and figures.
- **When will you use the material?** If you don't know now, you probably never will.
- **Is the information available elsewhere?** If it's on a computer disk, or somewhere else where you can find it easily when you really want it, then you don't need it in your files.
- **What would happen if you lost it?** If nobody would care, lose it.
- **Is the information strictly FYI?** Once you've read it, you can probably toss it without danger.

(*NewsClips*, Quill Corporation, Lincolnshire, IL)

Give life to boring memos

After you've written a memo but before you distribute copies, make it a habit to take a few minutes to go through the memo and mark it up. Jot a few words in the margin to clarify or emphasize; highlight key phrases in yellow. You'll personalize your inter-office communication, and make it easier to read, also.

Organize your time — it's as easy as A-B-C

Use your time more efficiently by classifying your tasks in terms of how quickly they need to be accomplished. You can do this by listing and then sorting them into three groups:

A. Tasks to be finished within seven days.
B. Jobs that should be completed by two weeks from today.
C. Long-term projects requiring a month or more of work.
And remember to update your lists daily!

(*American Fidelity Communicator*, 2000 Classen Center, Oklahoma City, OK 73106)

Cut down reading time with exception reports

Do you spend too much time reading reports that don't tell you anything new? Tell your subordinates to send you "exception reports" instead. An exception report should tell you what's going better than expected, what's going worse than anticipated, and how you can help. Save in-depth reports for occasions that really require a more substantial analysis: year-end performance reports, proposals for new sales promotions, and issues that can't be addressed in a single page or less.

(*The Better Association Manager*, cited in *The Effective Executive*, Dartnell, 4660 Ravenswood Ave., Chicago, IL 60640)

Hand out rolodex cards

Instead of carrying business cards, carry rolodex cards. When you hand them out at luncheons and meetings, people will be able to file them as soon as they return to their office.

Get organized, you'll be more productive

Clocks eventually catch up to culture; a nation that prides itself on productivity inevitably finds enough to keep it busy. When we reach even farther, we have to concoct ways to become more efficient so we can get even more work done. Maybe that's why we have digital watches that double as calculators. And it certainly explains Daily Planners and phone beepers and the whole range of modern tools.

Stephanie Winston's *The Organized Executive* fits right into our need to work faster, more efficiently, and more effectively. It gives you, for example, "Five Action Steps to Increased Productivity:"

■ Record in a single notebook every idea, assignment, call, project, task, or errand — large or small, minor or important — as it arises.

■ Review this Master List daily. Eliminate the non-essential; delegate chores that can be handled by others; defer those tasks that don't require immediate attention.

■ Compile tomorrow's Daily List. List and rank 10 things you accomplish in a single day.

■ Evaluate Daily List tasks in terms of likely payoff. When you're busy, you have to establish priorities. You can't afford to be working on something of minor significance when a project promising far greater results lies idle.

■ Determine prime time. Slot priority choices into this time, reserving other hours for less vital business. These prime hours may be decided on the basis of an individual's own work system, plus the availability of personnel and services.

The text also includes lists of work you can do in limited periods of time:

• **Five minutes:** Schedule an appointment, prepare a meeting attendance list, write a short note or dictate a short letter.

• **Ten minutes:** Make a few brief phone calls, proofread a short report, jot down meeting agenda notes, or order tickets for an upcoming event.

• **Thirty minutes:** Outline a report, read and mark up a report, skim magazine articles, organize and file papers.

Everybody devises their own methods of handling time, but this book will help you evaluate your techniques and see if you can make any improvements.

(Stephanie Winston, *The Organized Executive*, Warner Books, Inc., 666 Fifth Ave., New York, NY 10103)

Keep a diary

A diary is good for listing future dates and recording past ones. It should list whom you have lunch and dinner with — and where; your T&E expense items, advances, flight and train numbers, departures, arrivals, the names of hotels and restaurants you stay and dine at, and the names of plays and sports events you have taken clients to. Also, keep a record of key birthdays, wedding anniversaries, and the like.

Keeping a diary will be helpful when writing expense accounts. File them for future reference in case the IRS asks for a backup.

(*50 Rules to Keep a Client Happy*, by Fred Poppe)

Change your work habits

Each day make it a habit to read your mail and act on it. Quickly scan the letter or announcement; if the subject is irrelevant to your activities, quickly throw it away.

For responses, use fastest method possible:
1. Answer by telephone if feasible, then discard the letter.
2. Write a short note by hand on the original and return letter with answer.
3. If a formal answer is necessary, write or dictate the answer to be mailed the same day.

(*Games Mother Never Taught You*, by Betty Lehan Harragan, Warner Books, New York, NY; $14.95)

Rubber stamp it

If you have to write anything more than five times a day, don't. Get a rubber stamp.

So many pieces of in-house information produced by a business writer must be identified by your name or the name of your department, or the use to which the writing is to be put. A rubber stamp performs this function perfectly.

Practical business tips

☐ **Be assured** that your mail will be processed quickly if you print the zip code in bold numerals. Remember: The people at the post office sort through hundreds of thousands of letters a day using the zip code as a key.

(William Graham, Graham & Associates, P.O. Box 8711, Waukegan, IL 60079-9711)

☐ **Many times** the person writing you a letter forgets to include his or her address. So make it a habit to check the letter for a return address before throwing away the envelope.

(*The Secretary's Friend* by Anne Morton, Lown Publishing, Torrance, CA 90504; 256 pages, $12.95)

Use extra time productively

Extra time on your hands? Try some of these ideas:

- Organize your workspace. Clean your desk, put books away, discard old files you're sure you won't need anymore. Catch up on your paperwork.
- Review your computer files. A hard disk overloaded with unused files can slow down your computer. Be careful not to erase anything you might need in the future.
- Update your file of professional accomplishments. Keep a list of your duties and achievements on the job. This helps at performance review time. If you have trouble remembering what you did on a project six months ago, your supervisor won't recall easily, either.

(*Glaxo Ink*, Five Moore Dr., Research Triangle Park, NC 27709)

Guaranteed — You'll never forget a thing

Use the "Daily Prompter" reminder system and your life will be organized forever.

Your *Daily Prompter* can be a series of large envelopes, files, hanging file folders, binders, drawers, or boxes (shoe boxes wold be perfect).

If you use shoe boxes, label each box with a number from 1 to 31; and then label 12 others with calendar months. You'll need 43 in all.

How do you use your Daily Prompter? Some examples:

☐ **When you make an appointment** for a haircut next Tuesday, just drop yourself a note about the appointment in your *Daily Prompter* for next Tuesday's date.

☐ **Suppose you have a car payment** to make on the twentieth of every month. Put your payment book in your *Daily Prompter* sometime before the twentieth to remind you.

☐ **A meeting to attend** on the tenth and you want to bring important papers with you? Put those papers in your filing system, then drop yourself a note in your *Daily Prompter* about where you put them and what you want to do with them.

You can make better decisions by using your Daily Prompter.

☐ **For example:** You get a mailing piece urging you to buy a stereo system for $889 and you very much want to send away for it. Fill out the form, address the envelope, then put it in your Daily Prompter a week ahead. When it comes up again, look it over. It may not be so attractive anymore. But if it is, drop it in the mail (the paperwork will already be done.)

☐ **Use your monthly** *Daily Prompters* **for long-term projects.** Maybe you've decided to read three plays by Shakespeare in two months. Make a reminder of that goal, put it in the July Daily Prompter and, when it comes around, you can see whether you've met your goal or not.

(*How to Organize Your Work and Your Life*, Robert Moskowitz; Doubleday & Company, Inc., Garden City, New York; $9.95)

Color code your files

How many times have you sorted through mounds of paper work without finding the item you wanted? To save time try color-coding your files. Some suggestions:

Red: referred to once or more a day — store within arm's reach.

Green: referred to once a week or more — store within two steps of your chair.

Blue: referred to once a month or more — store outside your office where you can retrieve it as necessary.

Yellow or white: referred to once a year or more — store in a separate file room with an index to help you locate items you have "forgotten" that you have.

(*How to Organize Your Work and Your Life*, by Robert Moskowitz; Doubleday & Company, Inc.; $9.95)

Keep envelopes at your side

If someone calls asking for information about you or your company, write his or her address directly onto an envelope. That way you won't have to write the address twice.

(Tom O'Connor, St. Anne's Church, Hazel Crest, IL 60642)

Estimate your writing time

Do you underestimate the time it takes to write a report or memo? Many people do because they forget to include the time it takes to research, type, revise, edit, and copy their material. Here are some time estimates to help you meet your deadlines:

- **Allow four hours** per page for a complex assignment that requires several associates' approval.
- **Allow two hours** per page for a less complex report on a subject you are already knowledgeable about.
- **Allow an hour** for an important memo.

(*Put it in Writing*, by Jonathon Price, Viking Penguin, Inc., 40 W. 23rd Street, New York, NY 10010, and cited in *Glamour*, 350 Madison Ave., New York, NY 10017)

Write number bigger than usual

If you use a rolodex card in the form of a business card, give consideration to printing the telephone number about three times as big as your company's name and address. *Benefit:* it's a novelty that people will remember, and it puts your prospects with over-40 vision in a good mood before you even answer the phone.

(Jackson Trotter, 6000 42nd Ave., #404, Hyattsville, MD 20781)

Don't use two calendars

Two calendars are not necessarily better than one. If you have a desk calendar, and an organizer or appointment book, you might accidentally schedule two appointments at the same time. Instead, buy just one calendar — small enough to fit in your briefcase or purse — and carry it with you at all times.

(*Fortune*, Time Inc., 10880 Wilshire Blvd., Los Angeles, CA 90024-4193)

Avoid lengthy meetings

If a colleague wants to speak with you but you're pressed for time, try these tips for shorter conversations:

☐ Whenever possible, meet in his or her office instead of yours. Then, you will avoid having to dismiss your visitor. Instead, you can excuse yourself, saying something like, "Well, I can see you have a lot of work to do. I won't keep you any longer."

☐ Stand up when a colleague enters your office and remain standing. The other person will be less apt to sit down and chat.

(*Working Woman*, Hal Publications Inc., 342 Madison Ave., New York, NY 10173)

Time is money, so don't waste time

Some ways to save time:

In a memo, cover only one point. If you must cover more, number the points.

Take the lunch hour to do your writing. While everybody else is eating, you'll have more of the office to yourself and fewer telephone calls.

Include a photocopy of the letter you are sending to somebody. Use a rubber stamp that says, "To save time, send your reply on the back of the enclosed photocopy."

Don't waste time on the phone. "What can I do for you" is a pleasant way to begin talking business, even when an old acquaintance calls. "I'll let you go now," is a convenient way of signaling an end to the conversation. Another way is the simple fact: "I have to go now."

More ideas? You can get 166 time-saving ideas in a simple, readable, and free pamphlet by writing the publishers of *Execu-Time*, P.O. Box 631, Lake Forest, IL 60045.

Add mileage to trips

If you travel frequently on business, post your departure and return dates and destinations on a small calendar outside your office. Update the calendar two months in advance.
- Group planners can schedule meetings to include you.
- Coworkers can give you advance notice on group projects.
- Workers in other departments can inform you of key business contacts in the cities you're visiting.

Avoid 'drop-ins'

If interruptions of the "drop-in" variety plague your workday, maybe the problem is in your perspective — literally. Turn your desk to avoid eye contact with the hall outside your office door. When people have to work to get your attention, it's less likely they'll try in the first place.

Keep track of time spent

Each time you pick up the same piece of paper, put a small check mark on a corner. A row of check marks signals you've wasted too much time on the subject.

(*Hi Lites*, Hampton University, Office of University Relations, Hampton, VA 23668)

Publicize your hours

If you are available only at certain times of the day or if you don't want to accept calls at a certain time of the day, print your office hours on your stationery. For example: if you are available only from 11 p.m. to 2 p.m., put these hours next to your address and telephone number.

TIPS FROM READERS

Readers of *Bottom Line Communicator* are an unusually savvy lot. Not only are they always looking for new ideas in the publication, but they have a lot of bright ideas of their own. Here's a several-page sampling of the kinds of suggestions they volunteer.

- **File everything—so you won't lose documents.** Putting a memo or other documents somewhere on your desk to review when you have time practically guarantees its disappearance.

(Joan Schiffer, Public Relations Director, Ferndale Public Schools, 725 Pinecrest Drive, Ferndale, MI 48220)

- **Newswriters, make it easy on your readers:** when you refer to a person at the end of your story who was mentioned only briefly at the beginning, identify that person again: "Smith, the security guard."

(Elizabeth Saul, Manager of Office Operations, University of Chicago Graduate School of Business, 620 S. Ellis, Chicago, IL 60637)

- **When interviewing someone with a tape recorder,** don't laugh raucously at a humorous remark, because that's all you'll get on the tape and not the words your subject might add.

(Bob Dedinsky, 220 12th Ave., E., Seattle, WA 98102)

- **Before buying software for your computer,** check to make sure the company is reputable. Fly-by-night companies are making cheap software that can ruin your machine.

(Alima Mosquera, The Business Center, Palmer House, 17 E. Monroe St., Chicago, IL 60603)

- **When you're giving a speech,** attach a tiny digital clock to the lectern. This action will eliminate the need to look at your watch while trying to keep the speech within limits.

(Tom Berger, 135 Lawton, Riverside, IL 60546)

- **Save space in your publication** by reducing the table of contents (often a formality in thin magazines) to a boxed item on Page 2.

(Jeanne Barry, 901 S. Plymouth Ct., Chicago, IL 60605)

- **Check your paper tray.** Before making multiple copies on the xerox machine, check to make sure there is enough paper in the paper tray. This action won't necessarily save time, but it will stop you from damning the machine out loud when the paper tray empties.

(Edward Chesko, 67 E. Walworth Ave., Delevan, WI 53115)

- **Calculator can be quicker.** It's quicker to use the calculator when reducing picture sizes rather than the archaic proportion wheel.
    Here's how:
 1. Measure width of column you want picture to fit.
 2. Divide that measurement by width of picture and that will give you the percentage of picture that should be printed.
 3. To get the column length of photo, multiply percentage of picture by length of photo.

(Valerie Cihylik, 315 W. 102nd St., New York, NY 10025)

- **Identify yourself on every page.** Any kind of marketing letter or promotional package should have your name, address, and phone number printed on every page. *Why?* If a customer loses part of it, he or she will still be able to order your product. The best place to put your address is either at the top or foot of each page.

(Mindy Hutchinson, 920 N. Ridgeland, Oak Park, IL 60302)

- **How about free advice?** Call the "Grammar Hotline" when you have a question about word usage. Should you use *effect* or *affect*? Whatever the question, the people at the Grammar Hotline know the answer. Call Grammar Hotline Directory Writing Center, Tidewater Community College, 1700 College Crescent, Virginia Beach, VA 23456. Telephone: (804) 427-7170.

- **How many words per minute?** If you have to give a speech, remember that 170 words on a page equal one minute's talking time.

(*Spirit*, East/West Network, Inc., 34 E. 51st St., New York, NY 10022)

- **When giving a presentation,** place your notes on a table and stand at least 2 feet behind the table. This allows you to glance at your notes and look at your audience at the same time—without tilting your head downward.

(Judith S. Pruitt, Wordsmart, Inc., 1255 University Ave., Rochester, NY 14450)

- **Create a speech idea file.** Any time you see an article related to your field, clip it and create a file. The next time you're asked to speak, you'll have ideas on hand.

(Sisi Mosquera, 4707 N. Albany, Chicago, IL 60625)

- **Turn your business card into an advertisement.** George Plimpton, editor and publisher of *Paris Review*, puts a tiny order blank for a subscription to his magazine on the back of his business card.

- **Use the back of a new acquaintance's business card** to record important points about your first meeting. *For example:* You can record the date, place, mutual friends, topics discussed, etc., for future reference.

(Dale C. Enflish, West Seneca, NY)

- **The next time you are plagued with writer's block** and are staring at a blank page, write as if you're writing to a friend. Begin the rough draft with, "Dear ...."

(Chip Burke, Human Resource Representative, 1135 Norbert Lane, St. Paul, MN 55116)

- **Do you want your memo to be noticed?** Write the recipient's name by hand, in a bright color, at the top right instead of typing it in the usual place.

(Irene Goldman, Maxima Press, 517 S. Jefferson St., Chicago, IL 60607)

- **If you want to measure confidence in a letter,** follow this rule: The longer the memo, the less confident the sender. Conversely, the more succinct the memo, the more confident the sender.

(Edward Wakin, *Today's Office*)

- **Use short sentences when writing speeches.** *Why*? That's the way people talk. And it's far easier for listeners to understand your thoughts in short chunks than in long sentences with all manner of dependent clauses and perfect participles.

(Jim Sellers, 1730 Minda Drive, Eugene, OR 97401)

- **Focus your directory ad on why your company is better** than the competition. Remember: When customers pick up a business directory, they've usually made the decision to buy a product or service. Your ad must persuade them to buy that product or service from you.

    If possible, place ads in geographical listings as well as in product or service categories. Customers are just as likely to look for a business that is close to home as they are to check product listings.

- **If your company frequently hires temporary help,** put together an orientation booklet to familiarize workers with office procedures, standard letter formats, important names and phone numbers, and commonly used acronyms.

- **Whenever you delegate a project to someone,** mark it down in a "delegation book." Then, follow up on the project periodically. Using this system may help prevent those last-minute surprises like incomplete or forgotten projects that can mean disaster.

- **When you start a relationship with a new client,** send that person a welcome package to mark the occasion. Include a personal letter from your company president thanking the client for the business, and provide a guide to your company and its services. Be sure to include Telex, facsimile, and telephone numbers.

- **Make sure everyone on your staff** knows the names of your 10 most important customers. The staff will feel more a part of the business and will know how to establish priorities when one of those 10 customers calls with a request.

- **Make it easy to take messages:** Tear off the back sheet of a Post-It pad and stick the pad to your telephone.

(Chris St. Aubin, Hotel Manager, 1407 W. Belden, Chicago, IL 60614)

- **A follow-up sales letter** should not begin with "It was a pleasure talking to you ..." It's a cliche that no one believes. Begin your letter with an original statement that makes your reader remember you. The same goes for the ending. *Don't say*: "I look forward to meeting you soon."

(Jack Trotter, 6000 42nd Ave., #404, Hyattsville, MD 20781)

- **Show interest in a client** by enclosing a newspaper or trade journal clipping that relates to something the two of you discussed.

(Charles J. Shields, 18004 Hood, Homewood, IL 60430)

- **When sending work to be photostated,** tape often-used type, logos, or design elements to whatever you're sending. You'll get the extra stats for free, and you'll have some in different sizes when you need them.

(Howard Munce, *Graphics Handbook*)

- **Direct mail design tip:** To separate those graphic designers who understand direct mail from those who don't, pretend you don't know what indicias or FIM marks are and ask them to please explain. If they can't, look elsewhere.

(Marguerita Weiss, writing in *Direct Marketing*)

- **Don't let paperwork pile up.** When answering letters, forget perfection. If you make a mistake while typing, don't begin the letter again; x-out the word and keep typing. Not only will this action save you time, it will personalize your letters.

(Eugene Earnshaw, 17525 S. 71st Court, Tinley Park, IL 60477)

- **Handle photos with care.** Don't attach a photograph to another piece of paper using a paper clip. The photo will retain the image of the clip and spoil its reproduction. Similarly, a hard-pointed pen should not be used on the reverse side of a photo.

(William P. Crusius, Graphic Conservation Co., 900 N. Franklin St., Chicago, IL 60610)

- **Free Hotline Directory on status of bills.** Write for the free *Legislative Hotline Directory*, which lists telephone numbers in 50 states that you can call to check on the status of a bill in the state legislature. Many are toll-free. Similar numbers can be called to determine the progress of bills in the U.S. Congress. Send a stamped and self-addressed business envelope to Government Research Service, 701 Jackson, Room 304, Topeka, KS 66603.

- **Free catalogue of inexpensive books:** The U.S. Government books catalogue features hundreds of new and popular government publications that are for sale. The books cover energy, history, health, space, science, vacations, and many other topics. Write to Free Catalogue, P.O. Box 37000, Washington, DC 20401.

- **Tips from the experts:** Need advice on how to read faster, make a speech, or write with style? International Paper offers a free collection of short, entertaining essays on the above subjects and others by such luminaries as Kurt Vonnegut, George Plimpton, and Bill Cosby. Write: International Paper, College Survival Kit, Dept. CAM, P.O. Box 954, Madison Square Station, New York, NY 10010.

- **New uses for stick-on notes:** Here are some suggestions for making use of those handy little stick-on notes:
  - **Affix them to newsletters** to remind subscribers that their subscription is about to expire.
  - **Attach them to order forms,** suggesting a best buy or promising a limited time bonus.
  - **Have them commercially printed** or consider using a rubber stamp. If you make just a few mailings, write them by hand for a personal touch.

(*The Direct Response Specialist,* P.O. Box 1075, Tarpon Springs, FL 34688)

- **An easy way to organize a feature story:** Write the headline first—then write the story to fulfill the head's promise. *For example:* "7 Ways to Work Smarter, not Harder." OK, now find the 7 ways.

(Lew Dawson, 660-0 Avenida Sevilla, Laguna Hills, CA 92653)

- **When sending information to customers,** send it in such a way that they're sure to remember you. A pizza company sends catalogs to customers in a pizza box.

(*ADC Exchange,* 4900 W. 78th St., Bloomington, MN 55435)

VIDEO & RADIO

It's not enough for a communicator to be thoroughly grounded in the area of print media. These days, we all need to have some familiarity with the electronic media, too. If you're not already involved with radio and TV—or even if you are, but think there's more for you to learn—take a look at this sample of what *The Working Communicator* has to offer.

Five uses for video annuals

Corporate annual reports are often regarded by shareholders as expensive bits of puffery. But *Video Monitor* newsletter reports an alternative: the video annual report.

A videotaped version of the print standby can be produced at comparable cost, according to the newsletter, and has the following uses:
1. Distribute copies to branch and regional offices for employee viewing.
2. Show the tape to groups of shareholders or analysts by videoconference or by mailing cassettes to viewing sites.
3. Use excerpts in public service messages on TV.
4. Offer footage to cable TV systems for public viewing.
5. Use footage in fund-raising presentations, exhibits, trade shows, or conferences.

(Communication Research Associates, Inc., 10606 Mantz Rd., Silver Spring, MD 20903)

Target your message with radio ads

Radio advertising, especially for non-profit organizations, can be highly effective because radio audiences usually belong to very specific ethnic, cultural, or age groups in particular locations.

Target your audience if you've got a cause to promote, whether you're trying to reach teenagers in the suburbs or legislators at your state capitol. "When people hear it on the radio, they think it's being broadcast all around," says media consultant Tony Schwartz. "They don't realize it's being narrow-cast, just to them."

Video: The perfect marketing tool

Marketing by video is becoming more popular. Scott Schenker, audio-visual specialist, recommends that you follow these four basic tips when using video as a marketing tool.

☐ **Define your message first.** "Video is a sales tool," Schenker says, "You must think through your sales message. What exactly do you want to say? How can video be used to support that message? What are the key points to be emphasized? If your message isn't clear, no amount of camera work or special effects will help."

☐ **Prepare a script.** "Typically, you have 10-12 minutes to communicate your message in a clear, concise manner," says Schenker. "Once you've defined your message, assemble the facts, write the script and get it approved. One of the biggest mistakes I see is shooting video pictures first, then trying to write the script. It doesn't work."

☐ **Schedule a videotaping session.** "The photographer begins by videotaping the raw visuals," says Schenker. "He or she will try different angles and lighting to capture the visuals, using the script as a guide. Experience is important. Sometimes, in an effort to save a few dollars someone will ask a friend with a home video camera to 'help.' While this approach may be fine for internal use, it is usually a mistake for a marketing tool. The video represents you and your company. You wouldn't ask your neighbor to stand in for you at a sales presentation, why ask him to do your video?"

☐ **Postproduction: The final touch.** "The editor focuses on key features and benefits, keeping the pace lively. This is also the stage where music and narration can be added."

(*ITW Update*, 8501 W. Higgins Rd., Chicago, IL 60631-2887)

WRITING TECHNIQUES

Yes, it's the basic skill of the communicator, but no one can claim to be a finished expert in writing; there's always something else to learn. A few of these tips may help you on the way to further improvement (or perhaps will be effective in training someone on your staff).

What to call the clergy

If you know the correct courtesy titles to use with the clergy, you are among the few who do. Remember that the Rev. Leonard Dubi in a second reference or in a direct address is *Father* Dubi if he is a priest. He is *Mr.* Dubi (or possibly *Dr.* Dubi) if he is a minister. And *Pastor* Dubi if he is a Lutheran minister. He is never *Rev.* Dubi.

Always be specific

Whenever possible, substitute specific, credible numbers for vague, subjective adjectives.

Not: She is a *moderate* smoker.
But: She smokes *three* cigarettes a day.

Not: He is a *fast typist*.
But: He types *100* words a minute.

(Writing consultant, and *BLC* workshop leader, Peter Jacobi)

The local librarian: There is no substitute

When you have to do market research, check on a competitor, or find some kind of information for your business, ask a librarian to help you.

Find out the names of all the librarians you'll be dealing with, then determine when their least busy hours are and call them at that time. You'll be amazed at the help you'll get and the information you can find if you have a librarian on your side.

(*Money Making Marketing*, by Dr. Jeffrey Lant, JLA Publications, 50 Follen St., Suite 507, Cambridge, MA 02138; 617-547-6372)

Don't clutter 'up' your writing

Don't clutter your writing with unnecessary prepositions. The word "up" for instance, is frequently tagged onto verbs that can stand alone:

Not: John will head up the committee.
But: John will head the committee.

Not: We must face up to the problem.
But: We must face the problem.

(*On Writing Well* by William Zinsser, Harper & Row Publishers, Inc., 10 East 53rd St., New York, NY 10022)

Handle your difficult PR topics the easy way
Writing about high-tech and other difficult-to-understand topics takes time. Why not make it easier on yourself?
- Find a person in your organization who can talk you through jargon and buzzwords — enabling you to translate them for your audience.
- Prevent technical people from rewriting your draft copy.
- Include diagrams and fact sheets with your news releases, publications, or memos.
- Define all the abbreviations you use.

(Joel Goldstein, writing in *Public Relations Journal*, 845 3rd Ave., New York, NY 10022)

Write non-stop to get yourself started
For your first draft of any writing, don't worry about spelling, punctuation, grammar, or even matters of fact. Forget all the rules. Just sit down and write non-stop. The idea is to keep putting words down on paper, even if you write nothing but "I don't know what to write" over and over again. Since it's only a rough draft, it doesn't matter if you know exactly where your writing is headed. Novelist E.L. Doctorow says: "Writing a book is like driving a car at night. You can only see as far as your headlights go, but you can make the whole trip that way."

(*Turbocharge Your Writing!* by Joe Vitale, P.O. 300792, Houston, TX 77230)

Remember WIIFM, WIIFT
Remember these two initialisms WIIFM ("What's In It For Me?") and WIIFT ("What's In It For Them?"). When you write a business letter or a report, or before your next presentation, ask yourself what your purpose is (WIIFM) and what you want your reader/audience to take away (WIIFT). This will help you clarify your thinking and communicate more effectively.

(Nancy Stern, quoted in *How to Write Like An Executive*, by Patricia H. Westheimer and Vickie Townsend Gibbs, Scott, Foresman and Company, Glenview, IL)

After you read a great story, file it
The best way to acquire anecdotes to illustrate points in articles or speeches is *not* to spend countless dollars on books (and countless hours reading them), but to use the stories you come across by chance. Type them on index cards and file them according to topic: Business, Education, Politics, Work, Miscellaneous, etc. If an anecdote fits in more than one category, file it more than once. Even when you're rushed, take a few minutes to record a great story — it'll save you hours later.

(Jim Sellers, *Capital Ideas for Speechwriters,* Capital Ideas Press, 1730 Minda Drive, Eugene, OR 97401)

Know when to use titles and when not to

Some reminders to writers and editors who also act as reporters for publications in organizations.

☐ <u>Don't use "I," "you," "we," etc. in a news story</u> unless it's an eyewitness account. It's "the Company," not "our Company." *Never:* "The speaker told us that...." *Instead:* "....the speaker told the audience." *Better yet:* "....the speaker said...."

☐ <u>Don't let titles cloud your narrative.</u> Common titles — Dr., Sen., the Rev., etc. — may be used at any time. But cumbersome, contrived titles should be avoided in first references. *Don't say:* "Second Assistant Vice-President in charge of Wastebaskets and Paperclips William Southby and First Deputy Investment Under-Treasurer Dorothy Connors attended the meeting." *Instead, write:* "William Southby and Dorothy Connors attended the meeting. He is ..., and she is ... etc."

Want 99 more tips? Ask us to send you (FREE) *101 Memos for Reporters —* guidelines on how to get the news and write the story. Write *The Working Communicator*, 407 S. Dearborn St., Chicago, IL 60605.

Avoid these cliches

Here are five words and phrases you should never use in any communication with employees:

Loyal and dedicated — the two words come together so often you'd think they were hyphenated.

Challenges and opportunities — same as above.

Played a key role — if so, recognize the achievement with original language.

Family — if the employees are a family, what does that make the CEO?

Pat on the back — often a patronizing substitute for meaningful recognition.

Writing tips that have stood the test of time

Here's some advice on how to communicate more effectively that is as timely today as when it was written 42 years ago.

■ Never use a metaphor, simile or other figure of speech which you are used to seeing in print.

■ Never use a long word where a short one will do.

■ If it is possible to eliminate a word, always do so.

■ Never use the passive where you can use the active.

■ Never use a foreign phrase, a scientific or jargon word if you can think of an everyday English equivalent.

■ Break any of these rules sooner than say anything outright barbarous.
The author? George Orwell, author of *1984* and *Animal Farm*.

("Politics and the English Language" by George Orwell, from *Shooting an Elephant and Other Essays*)

Self-help test: Are you a sexist writer?

	Yes	No
1. Do you describe the women you write about in greater physical detail than the men you write about?	☐	☐
2. Do you refer to adult women as "girls" or "gals" or "ladies" and consistently refer to adult males as "men"?	☐	☐
3. Do you routinely provide information about the marital status of women you write about but not the men?	☐	☐
4. Do you use "lady" as a modifier, as in "lady architect," "lady welder," and "lady lawyer"?	☐	☐
5. Have you ever written to a woman or introduced a woman using only her husband's name (Mrs. Brian Murphy)?	☐	☐
6. Do you call women by their first names and men in similar positions by their last names or last names and courtesy title?	☐	☐
7. Do you automatically begin a letter "Dear Sir"?	☐	☐
8. Do you exclude women from occupational categories by using words ending in -man (*businessman, congressman, repairman*)?	☐	☐

If you answered yes to any of the above questions, you can't dismiss out of hand the suggestion that sexism is coloring your writing. *The Working Communicator* is still giving away FREE helpful guidelines that can help writers deal with sexist language. To ask us to send them to you, write to us at: 212 W. Superior Street, Chicago, IL 60610.

Don't miscommunicate with sexist language

Unintentional sex bias often hides in pronouns, leaping out and offending those sensitive to such things. Judy E. Pickens, editor of *Without Bias: A Guidebook for Non-Discriminatory Communication*, offers these configurations:

1. **No pronoun.** "Each employee should check out before leaving for lunch."
2. **Plural pronoun.** "Employees should check out before you go to lunch."
3. **Second-person pronoun.** "You should check out before you go to lunch."
4. **Alternating pronouns.** "Each employee should check out before he or she goes to lunch."

Seventeen tips for employee publications

1. Write actively.
2. Stop trying to win a popularity contest in your publication.
3. Speak *with* your readers, not to them.
4. Always keep in mind the purpose of the publication.
5. Write about employees you would like your readers to imitate.
6. Don't go wild with color because your printer has a new, two-color press.
7. Put together a publication you feel good about.
8. Don't write a "holiday message."
9. Your publication is for your readers, to help them do their jobs better.
10. Get rid of the "grip-and-grin" photos — without feeling an ounce of guilt.
11. Think. Think about the information you receive for your publication.
12. Use common sense.
13. Write *about* employees, *for* employees.
14. Don't write a publication you wouldn't want to read.
15. Less is more. Don't put too much in the publication. Let one story, one photo, one employee stand for many.
16. Show management you are a communications expert, on whose judgment they can rely.
17. You didn't get where you are for lack of talent; believe in yourself.

(The Editors of *The Working Communicator*)

Write better story leads

Never begin a story using a dictionary definition of a word, like "Webster defines pride as ..." No one will continue reading. **One exception:** If you're defining something that has many definitions, give a dictionary definition, *then* the other definitions.

Check to see if you're following the issues

How much of your communication relates to the issues of your company? **Here's a perfect way to find out:** If you edit a company newsletter, go over the articles in your publications. Go back through the last 12 issues. Do a content analysis. Write down the subjects on paper. Now look at the problems/issues facing your company and write those down on another sheet. If the two sheets don't match, you probably aren't communicating with your readers, and it's time to make some changes.

(*Strategies For Business Communicators*, by Joe Williams, Communication Illustrated, P.O. Box 924, Bartlesville, OK 74005)

Headlines require single quotes
Many editors forget this rule: if you're quoting someone in a headline, remember that only single quotes enclose the phrase.

Rules for writing better news stories
- Don't assume that the reader knows the background of a story; leave no reasonable questions unanswered.
- Go directly to the primary source of a story. Every intermediate source confuses the account.
- Each paragraph of a story should blend naturally into the next one. There should be no interruption of the thought, no sharp jolt from one idea to another. When a story is well written, one phrase can't be deleted without injuring the whole story.
- Always write so the reader will say, "This could happen to me."
- Look up every quotation you use. Even if you are absolutely sure that Eve bit into the apple in the Garden of Eden before Adam did, you should still look it up in Genesis ... and find out there is no apple mentioned anywhere in that account. (It was just "fruit.") And Sherlock Holmes never said, "Elementary, my dear Watson."
- "Select adjectives as you would a diamond or a mistress," said Stanley Walker, editor of the old *New York Herald Tribune*, "too many are dangerous."

(*101 Memos for Reporters,* by Ed Arnold, 3208 Hawthorne, Richmond, VA 23222)

Quote of the month
There is no right way. Each of us finds a way that works. But there is a wrong way. The wrong way is to finish your writing day with no more words on paper than when you began. Writers write.

(*Robert Parker*)

Offer readers an incentive
If you must use an editor's note for a story, put it at the end. *Why?* If you put it at the beginning, it keeps the reader from plunging directly into the story. *One exception:* If the story is extremely controversial and requires an editor's note, put that at the beginning — it will quickly draw your reader into the story.

Use quotes as often as you can
If you write corporate prose, **remember:** people would rather read words with quote marks around them than the same words without the quote marks. Quotation shows authority, the human presence, and it breaks up type.

(Peter Jacobi, Professor of Journalism, University of Indiana, Bloomington, IN 47405)

Use the colon to eliminate words

To save space, don't hesitate to make frequent use of the colon. English teachers don't ordinarily preach the virtues of the colon, but its uses, evident to headline writers, can knock words out of your sentence. An example: "Forget what you learned in school about the colon. It can help you in many ways. One way: Its terseness helps you save words."

Just in case you're sued

Be consistent when saving material on stories you have worked on. Either save everything, save some elements, or save nothing, but be sure to do the same thing the same way every time. *Important consideration:* Legal opinion seems to be veering away from the "save everything" mentality. Editors, it's suggested, should be especially cautioned against writing comments and questions on manuscripts, a casual "what does this mean?" could come back at you in court.

(*Hotline*, Newsletter Association, 1401 Wilson Blvd., Suite 403, Arlington, VA 22209)

Editorial goals: Serving needs and wants

Every editor struggles with the question, "What do my readers want to know?"

This question is different from the statement: "My readers *need* to know...."

Editors in organizations must provide information that readers need, which will help the organization move forward. Yet if the publication contains nothing but need-to-know information it is in danger of boring and patronizing readers.

Remember: answer questions that readers are asking and you'll win the loyalty, even the affection of readers. The tension between need-to-know and want-to-know comes with the territory. Use it to serve your organization well.

Advice for writing about people with handicaps

When writing stories about people who are handicapped make sure to choose your words carefully. Much bias exists when handicapped people are described. Little City Foundation offers advice:

☐ Choose words that carry non-judgmental connotations and accurately describe the person. For example, it is appropriate to call the subject of a story "a person with a disability" or "an individual with a handicap." However, people are not conditions. They should not be lumped into such categories as "the disabled." They are people first and foremost.

☐ Calling people "retarded," "crippled," or "deformed" is judgmental. On the flipside, avoid using adjectives such as "courageous," "brave," and "inspirational" unless they truly reflect the person's character. Adapting and coping with a disability does not turn someone into Mother Teresa.

☐ Ask the person you interview to provide technical information about his or her handicap so that you will have an *accurate* description of the disability.

(Mark Gould, Little City Foundation, 4801 W. Peterson Ave., Chicago, IL 60646)

A variety of ways to cure writer's block

Speechwriter's Newsletter asked its readers what they do to overcome writer's block. Here are some of the remedies they found helpful, in their own words.

■ When I'm blocked, I usually pick up the *Philadelphia Inquirer* and just browse. Inevitably something catches my eye and starts the creativity flowing — even if it's a $19.95 oil change special.

■ Take a walk — take a swim — do something physical but private so I can relax *and* think!

■ I walk around and visit with my cohorts or page through my *Bartlett's Book of Quotations* to remind myself of the word's great writing and try to explain to myself why I'm not doing it.

■ If I'm stuck, it usually means I don't know something: the audience, the purpose of the occasion, my client's message or thoughts on the subject, key facts. When I find out what it is that I need to find out, I'm fine. The worst "block" experiences are always with jokes.

■ When possible, I bounce the ideas off someone else. Verbalizing my thoughts seems to put things into perspective, and before you know it, I'm off and writing.

■ Wait 24 or 48 hours if I have the time available. Otherwise write in a state of panic (at times with surprisingly good results).

■ When totally impaired, I do the most obvious: wait until the pressure to have copy by the deadline becomes so great, my mind, fingers, and creativity merge and explode in a streamlined jet spray of solid, usually pretty damn good prose.

■ Talking about it helps.

■ I prefer to crank up by writing anything, just to get something down. It's generally total garbage, but then I go through it, pick out the surprisingly "good" stuff. I take these nuggets and start to build around them. . . then I'm on a roll!

■ You have to write — anything at all — and it will loosen up the machinery. One writer I know just types obscenities, over and over, until the gears mesh and something else appears.

■ Hemingway always stopped in midstream, when he knew what was coming next. James Joyce and Gertrude Stein took long walks. Wallace Stevens wrote much of his poetry *while* he walked.

■ Listen to the radio — news or talk shows. Sometimes hearing someone reading helps me get a new twist on my writing.

■ Some people create visually, some mentally; we create with words. Writers don't start thinking about a subject seriously until we get the words down.

■ I write out a list of objectives. What do I want to tell this audience? Am I communicating a message, or persuading? What am I trying to say?

Editor's note: For a free sample copy of *Speechwriter's Newsletter*, write to: *Speechwriter's Newsletter,* 212 W. Superior, Street, Chicago, IL 60610.

Every masthead should tell facts
The masthead — the box in a publication with the details of publication — should have four pieces of information:
1. The name of the publisher or publishing organization
2. The name and title of the editor
3. The editor's complete phone number, including area code
4. The editor's complete mailing address, including zip

(*Editing the Organizational Publication*, 3208 Hawthorne, Richmond, VA 23222)

Notes without quotes
Take better notes by writing down your interpretation of the speaker's ideas, rather than verbatim quotes. The extra step will solidify the point in your mind.

Some gutsy ideas for editors
You'll have a winner if you edit your publication with these gutsy, zesty, feisty ideas, advanced by Richard Teresi, editor of *Omni* Magazine.
- Don't try to write for everyone. Write in the language that your readers know.
- Don't be afraid to offend people. Controversy builds interest and readership.
- Don't dilute the publication by trying to broaden its appeal.
- Don't read your competitor's publication. Let competitors adjust their style to yours.
- Don't worry about awards. Please your readers, not your peers.
- Don't be afraid to take strong stands.

(Richard Teresi, speaking at the 1988 annual publications management conference, sponsored by the *Society of National Association Publications* 3299 K St., NW, Washington, DC 20001)

Think of punctuation as signs along the road
Lovers of punctuation will rejoice in *Time* magazine's essay on the comma. Some highlights:
- Think of punctuation as road signs: a period is the red light; the comma is yellow, asking us to slow down; and the semicolon is "a stop sign that tells us to ease gradually to a halt."
- When the parent warns the child, there is a difference between "Don't do that" and the elimination of the contraction, spoken slowly — "Do not do that."
- Study the way the comma adds to a sentence from V.S. Naipul's latest novel: "He was a middle-aged man, with glasses." The comma "shows that the glasses are not part of the middle-agedness, but something else."
- "Punctuation, in short, gives us the human voice, and all the meanings that lie between the words."

Eight tips for researchers who take notes

Here are some suggestions to help you avoid confusion in your notetaking while doing research:
1. Use paper or cards of uniform size.
2. Have only one piece of information on any single card.
3. Label each card in the upper left-hand corner with a key word.
4. Use ink. Pencil marks will rub off or smudge.
5. Write down author, title, and page number on each card. This way you can make an accurate reference to the information immediately.
6. Never write on both sides of anything. That way you won't have to worry about missing anything you've noted.
7. Don't copy whole pages verbatim. If you want to use a long quote from something, make a photocopy of the page. You eliminate any chance of error.
8. Abbreviate — but make sure you abbreviate consistently.

(*Impact*)

Maybe it's time to break some rules

"Writing a memo while rigidly sticking to the teachings of your freshman English teacher can put you in a bind that thwarts both productivity and communication," advises Rond Dulek in *mgr*, the publication of Atlantic Richfield (515 S. Flower St., Los Angeles, CA 90071). We couldn't agree more with Dulek's attacks on pedantry. Writing is meant to communicate, not to force obedience to abstract rules. If breaking a rule helps you communicate, break it. Or, as Dulek advises, feel free to break the following rules:

Never begin a sentence with "and," "or," "but," "nor," or "for." This rule started only because instructors wanted students to combine sentences in an age when complexity, following the Latin, was prized. In reality, begin with anything you want to make your point most clearly and effectively.

Avoid simple sentences. Don't confuse the simple with the simplistic. Much complex writing masks weak thought, and a stunning idea is often written in brief, striking prose: *I am not an animal, I am a man.*

Never use a one sentence paragraph. "Why not?" asks Dulek. If one sentence does the job, use one sentence and move on to the next paragraph.

Always be brief. Don't confuse brevity with conciseness. Conciseness is our goal, saying what we want to say in as few words as possible. Conciseness doesn't mean, *per se*, fewer words, just the fewest possible to do the job. But sometimes the job requires a lot of words, particularly for the novel, the complex, and the technical.

Never end a sentence with a preposition. If you follow this rule slavishly, you'll find your writing becoming stilted. What is wrong with this sentence: *The XYZ case is one that the AA rules apply to.* Nothing.

The perfect question
During interviews the best question to ask is often the last one. Ask: *Is there anything you think is important that I haven't asked?* This question ends the interview and often the answer is packed with information you wouldn't have dreamed of getting.

(*The Craft of Interviewing*, by John Brady)

Guidelines for proper use of trademarks
- Trademarks are proper adjectives and need to be followed by a generic noun or product description the first or most prominent time they appear, and at least once on every page.
- Trademarks need to be distinguished from other words by using an initial capital letter, all capital letters, italics, boldface, or color.
- Trademark status should be shown by using either ® for registered marks or tm for unregistered marks the first or most prominent time a trademark appears, and at least once on every page.
- Trademarks should not be used in the possessive form.
- Trademarks should not be used in the plural form.
- Trademarks should not be connected to another word by a hyphen or any other mark of punctuation.
- Trademarks cannot be followed by the ® symbol unless they have been registered in the U.S. Patent Office.

(*Hercules Horizons*, Hercules Inc., Hercules Plaza, Wilmington, DE 1984)

Avoid 'echo quotes' and other awkward errors
City Councilman John Jones said today he would quit drinking after being arrested for driving under the influence of alcohol last night. "I'll quit drinking," Jones said.

What's wrong with the preceding paragraph? The second sentence is an "echo quote." The writer has already told us that Jones is going to stop drinking in the first sentence, so repeating that in a quote just wastes the reader's time. In this situation, either work the quote into the lead sentence or find a different quote to use.

The City Council passed a resolution reprimanding Councilman John Jones "for failing in his responsibility to set a good example to the community."

The problem here? Documents should normally be paraphrased, not quoted, unless the document is the whole thrust of the story. You may need to dig, but you should always be able to find people to quote in a story.

Mayor Sam Smith loudly demanded Councilman Jones' "immediate resignation" in a press conference this morning.

Try to avoid quotes that are only two or three words long; paraphrase them if necessary.

Use the Fog Index to measure readability

Is your report too complex for the average reader? One way to measure its readability is with the "Fog Index." First, determine the average number of words per sentence. Then, count the average number of three-syllable words per hundred words of copy. Add these two totals, multiply by .04, and you've got the grade level required to read the material without any difficulty. The *Wall Street Journal*'s Fog Index is approximately 11, meaning that you don't even need to be a high school graduate to read it easily.

(Colin Hayes, *A Guide to Successful Public Relations,* Scott, Foresman & Co., Glenview, IL)

Who you gonna call? Grammar Hotline!

Hopefully, you can find out what's wrong with this sentence by calling your local grammar hotline. For a FREE directory of the grammar hotlines in the United States and Canada, write to: Grammar Hotline Directory, Tidewater Community College Writing Center, 1700 College Crescent, Virginia Beach, VA 23456.

Read the whole story when writing headlines

Don't read just the lead sentence when you write a headline for your publication. Many times the writer's real point becomes clear only later in the story. If you read the story completely, you'll be able to write a headline that will reflect the story as a whole, not just the first paragraph.

Eight tips for better advertising

1. Put your most important customer benefit in the headline.
2. Get the word "Free" into your headline or subheadline.
3. Provide an 800 phone number for orders, or accept collect calls.
4. Place a time limit on your offer.
5. Tell your reader to call, write, or order NOW — say it several times.
6. Use a perforated coupon, or some other kind of detachable reply device.
7. Put yourself in the reader's shoes.
8. Start your reply device with a restatement of your biggest customer benefit.

(*SOURCEfile*, P.O. Box 9280, Phoenix, AZ 85068-9280)

Include photos, dateline with writing samples

Sending out copies of your published writing? Don't send just the story itself — include any photos that might have run with the piece, and the dateline. The pictures will strengthen your sample, and the dateline will identify the piece and place it in context.

Interviewing the CEO: Five questions to ask
☐ Who are your heroes?
☐ If you were a college freshman and wanted to be president of the company some day, what would you study for the next four years?
☐ If you could have any job other than your own, what would it be?
☐ What's your typical day like?
☐ If you were one of our customers, what one thing would you like to see us doing differently?

Speed up the clearance process
Getting superiors to clear your writing can be a chore in itself. When you ask for clearances:
- Ask only those people directly involved with the story being cleared. Don't ask for general or departmental clearances.
- Request — and accept — clearances only on matters of fact — never style.
- Start the clearance process as high as possible and work down, using a routine slip. People are less likely to correct the ideas of a superior.
- Give unreasonable deadlines. If your deadline is Friday, ask for the copy by Tuesday. On the clearance slip, write: "If I don't hear from you by Tuesday, I'll assume everything is O.K."
- Have your clearance process in writing; make it a matter of policy.

(*Editor's Workshop, The newsletter that will help improve your publication,* 212 W. Superior Street, Chicago, IL 60610.)

Twelve ideas for your next annual report
1. Include a coupon for one of your products.
2. Leave one page blank for readers' notes.
3. If possible, include your product — a sample of your paper, a small computer disk, a greeting card — if it will fit.
4. Feature your employees or customers on the cover. Let a constituent other than an investor present the report.
5. Leave plenty of white space — half on each text page, at the least.
6. Describe your organization — locations, number of employees, products, customers — on the inside front cover.
7. Give your CEO's message its own specific headline. Make "A letter to shareholders" an overline, or kicker.
8. Place more emphasis — use more space — on the future than on the past.
9. Send your social responsibility report and employee annual report along with your corporate annual report.
10. Avoid the opening, "It was the best of times," etc.
11. Make financial graphs dramatic by using perspective — break out of two-dimensional pie charts and bar graphs.
12. Note your organization's age on the cover: "The 130th annual report of..."